# MAKE IT BY THE BOOK

This edition published by Parragon Books Ltd in 2016

Parragon Books Ltd
Chartist House
15–17 Trim Street
Bath BA1 1HA, UK
www.parragon.com

Crafts by Rachael Fisher, Kat Roberts and Kate Woods
Edited by Becky Wilson and Grace Harvey
Designed by Rachael Fisher and Karissa Santos
Stock photography by Shutterstock and iStock
Production by Charlene Vaughan
Designed, produced and packaged by Rachael Creates

ISBN 978-1-4723-9211-4

Printed in China

# MAKE IT BY THE BOOK

## PaRragon

Bath · New York · Cologne · Melbourne · Delhi
Hong Kong · Shenzhen · Singapore · Amsterdam

# CONTENTS

# INTRODUCTION

Get ready to unleash your creativity with over 80 ideas for going craft-crazy!

What's crafting? It's creating, inventing, recycling and upcycling all rolled into one! It's making something new from something old. It's making something new from something new. It's MAKING something.

Be inspired by the things around you! Turn toilet rolls into an Advent calendar, odd socks into coat hook ninjas, and empty cardboard boxes into a full-on castle.

So what are you waiting for? Have a go, experiment, try something new and get crafting!

## SAFETY AND ADULT SUPERVISION

Some crafts may require an adult to help, such as when using hot items (oven, hot water, glue gun or hairdryer) and sharp tools (craft knife), as well as using a sewing machine or hanging up fixtures on walls to showcase your creations. There will be prompts in the 'Materials' lists to remind you to ask for help, so look out for the * signs!

# TOOLS AND MATERIALS

Arm yourself with some basic craft supplies, so you're ready to get creative whenever you want!

## DRAWING, CUTTING, MEASURING AND MORE!

Pencils, marker pens, pens, rulers, paintbrushes, scissors, craft knives and measuring tapes are all essential tools to have around. Some crafts may suggest using a specific tool, but you can always alter the craft if you don't want to splash out on something new. ⌐→

coloured and patterned paper

tracing paper

tissue paper

crepe paper

white paper

card

## PAPER AND CARD

There are many different types of paper and card available, from tissue paper to patterned gift wrap, and card sheets to cardboard boxes. Stock up on some essentials and have fun making things like origami birds, crepe paper skirts and even cardboard castles! ⌐

## FABRICS, FELT AND FOAM

Most of the makes in this book use lightweight fabrics. Others include canvas fabric – a heavy-duty material perfect for hard-wearing makes. Felt and foam sheets are easy to cut and glue, and felt can even be sewn! ⌐→

felt

craft foam

patterned fabric

canvas

duct tape

washi tape

masking tape

## TAPE

Washi tape comes in lots of colours and patterns, so it's great for decorating and creating big pieces of art. It's also easy to remove if you change your mind! Masking tape is an all-purpose tape, while duct tape is brightly coloured and long-lasting. ⌐

measuring tape
ruler
compass
scissors
eraser
paintbrush
black pen
pencil
craft knife
marker pen

white glue (PVA)
glue stick
all-purpose glue (adhesive)
glue gun

# GLUES

White glue (PVA) is ideal for most basic crafts, glue sticks are mess-free but mainly used with paper, glue guns are great for card, fabric, plastic and wood, while all-purpose glues (adhesives) are fab on almost anything!

* Always ask an adult to help when using all-purpose glue and glue guns. Check safety labelling before use.

# COLOUR

As well as coloured pencils, acrylic paints and poster paints, experiment with other mediums to colour your masterpieces. Make a picture from melted wax crayons, colour flowers with nail polish or decorate a lampshade using highlighter pens. Be brave and get creative!

wax crayons
coloured pencils
paints
highlighter pens
fabric pens
nail polish
food colouring
fabric paint

wool
ribbon
string
thread
jewellery wire
twine
embroidery thread

# STRINGS AND THINGS

Thread, wool, string, twine and ribbon can be used in many ways. Whether you're stitching material together, knitting something to wear or hanging up decorations, keep these must-have items somewhere to hand. If you're mad about jewellery, invest in some jewellery wire (and cutters) too!

# HOUSEHOLD STUFF

Everyday objects can easily be upcycled and recycled into fabulous creations, like a glove octopus, a hairgrip necklace or a juice carton money box. So, before you bin it, think how to treasure it!

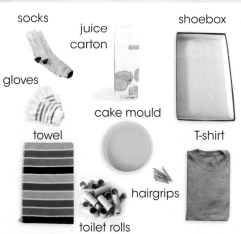

socks
juice carton
shoebox
gloves
cake mould
towel
T-shirt
hairgrips
toilet rolls

11

# TIPS AND TECHNIQUES

Try out different craft-making techniques to gain new skills and take your creations to another level.

## MANUFACTURING INSTRUCTIONS

Some crafts may suggest using a specific type of material that also comes with its own instructions. Make sure you read these carefully before you begin. There will be prompts in the 'Materials' lists to remind you to ask for help, so look out for the * signs!

running stitch

backstitch

stretch stitch

cross-stitch

## SEWING

This book explores a few basic hand-stitching techniques. If you're unsure how to do them, ask an adult to help or to show you video tutorials online. Some crafts also suggest using a sewing machine. Although this is a great timesaver, all of the makes in this book can be hand-stitched if preferred.

## KNOTS

These are mainly used to secure a craft or for adding on stitches (as in crochet). Look at these basic knots and practise them so you're familiar with the techniques inside.

The reef knot is also known as a double knot.

slip knot                    double (reef) knot

loop 1

1.

loop 1

loop 2

2.

feed loop 2 through loop 1

3.

pull tight

4.

1.

2.

3.

4.

slip knot – a type of knot used at the start of crocheting

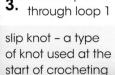

chain – a type of crochet stitch

treble crochet – a type of crochet stitch

Turn to pages 172–175 to learn more about crochet.

working wool – the wool connected to the ball of wool

tail – the loose end of the wool

## CROCHETING AND KNITTING

We only use a few crochet stitches in this book (shown far left), but if you've never crocheted before, don't worry. Ask an adult to help you or to show you video tutorials online so you can master the basics first. See pages 26–29 for knitting.

shrink plastic

washi tape

clock mechanism

craft beads

fabric pens

fabric paints

# ORIGAMI

Originally associated with Japanese culture, origami is the art of paper folding. If you find some of the steps a bit tricky in this book, ask an adult to help or to show you some online video tutorials. You'll soon be fabulous at folding!

↵

# QUILLING

Quilling, or paper filigree, involves rolling, curling, twisting, looping, shaping and gluing together strips of paper to create a design. Paper coils are curled more quickly and easily with a quilling tool than they are by hand, so it might be worth investing in this special tool if you like quilling. └→

1.

2.

3.

4.

# PRINTING

Everyday objects can make great stamping tools, such as kitchen utensils, buttons, bubble wrap, toilet rolls and more. Look around your home and see if you can find anything that could create a perfect print too.

↵

# TOP TIPS

As with anything, practice makes perfect. The more you make, the better you'll get and the faster you'll go! You'll also pick up some top tips that can be used on other crafts too. Try these handy hints (shown right) in your craft making.*

* Ask an adult for help! └→

To make a central hole in a piece of card (or paper), place a blob of sticky tack at the back and wiggle a pencil through into the tack.

To help card bend more easily, lightly score it first using scissors (or a craft knife) and a metal ruler.

# BEAD-IFUL
# BOWL

**EASY BEAD-Y!**

paper towel

oven-proof bowl

MATERIALS ↰

kitchen oil

small, fusible
plastic beads*

How do itty bitty beads keep all your odds and ends safe? Just melt them together to make a fabulous bead bowl. Now that's crafty!

* Beads must be suitable for craft making and use with an iron or oven!

**1.** Preheat the oven to 200°C.* Then pour a few drops of oil into the bowl. This will help the beads to stick to the sides in step 3.

* Ask an adult to do this!

**2.** Use a paper towel to spread the oil evenly around the bowl. Make sure you cover the whole area, otherwise the beads might not stay in place.

**3.** Press the beads against the insides of the bowl to form a single layer all around. Create a pretty pattern by alternating the colours in each row!

**4.** Place the bowl on a baking tray and put it in the oven for 10 minutes.* Keep an eye on the beads, as they may take less or more time to melt together.

* Ask an adult to do this for you.

**5.** When all the beads have melted, take the bowl out of the oven and leave to cool for 15 minutes.

**6.** Finally, carefully tip the melted beads out of the bowl. They should now be a bowl shape too!

17

RO-BOX BOWLING

STRIKE!

Create a fab robot bowling game. Turn empty boxes into dangerous droids, then line 'em up and knock 'em down. The player who strikes the most robots with the ball is the winner!

**MATERIALS**
tall, narrow, empty food boxes x 10, coloured paper, pencil, ruler, tape, scissors, glue stick, compass, black pen, ball

**1.**
Choose a box, then tape it down to ensure all sides are shut and secure.

**2.**
Draw around the base of the box onto a piece of paper.

**3.**
Now add a tab to each side of the square. Measure 3 cm from each corner to create four rectangular tabs. Carefully cut around the tabs.

**4.**
Repeat the steps so you have two matching shapes. Add glue to one side of each shape.

**5.**
Place the base of the box on one of the shapes, as shown.

**6.**
Fold and press the rectangular tabs to stick them to the box. Now glue the other shape to the top of the box.

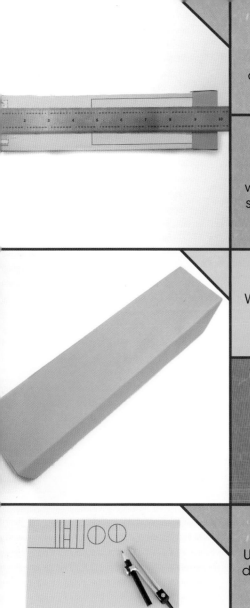

## 7.
When the top and base of the box are covered in paper, use your ruler to measure the length of the box.

## 8.
Cut out a piece of paper the same length as the box, making sure it is wide enough to wrap around all four sides. Add 3 cm extra to the width to make a tab.

length of box

side 1 | side 2 | side 3 | side 4 | tab

width of box | 3 cm

## 9.
Wrap and glue the paper to the box, completely covering any original packaging design.

## 10.
Repeat the previous steps using the rest of your empty boxes and coloured paper to make ten 'pins'.

## 11.
Using your ruler, compass and pencil, draw different-sized rectangles, circles and semicircles on the coloured paper to make the heads, arms, bodies and legs of the robots.

## 12.
Now cut out all the pieces.

## 13.
Create each robot character using the cut-out pieces of paper. Glue them to one side of a box, then draw the face, buttons and dials using black pen.

## 14.
Repeat step 13 for all the other boxes and then you are ready to play

# RO-BOX BOWLING!

patterned washi tape

plain gift tags

scissors

jars

**MATERIALS**

Originating in Japan, washi tape is a special kind of tape that's colourful, multi-patterned and easy to use. It's great for upcycling everyday items, like old jars. Try this super-simple craft and make some sweet gifts for friends and family!

1. Thoroughly clean out the jars before you start.*

2. Choose the washi tape patterns, then stick the tape on the jars. Experiment with vertical, horizontal or diagonal designs. Cover the jars with tape or leave an area clear to reveal the tasty treats inside.

3. When you've finished, fill the jars with wrapped sweets.

4. Decorate the gift tags to match each jar's unique design, then tie them on!

* Ask an adult to clean the jars in a dishwasher or with hot water and washing-up liquid.

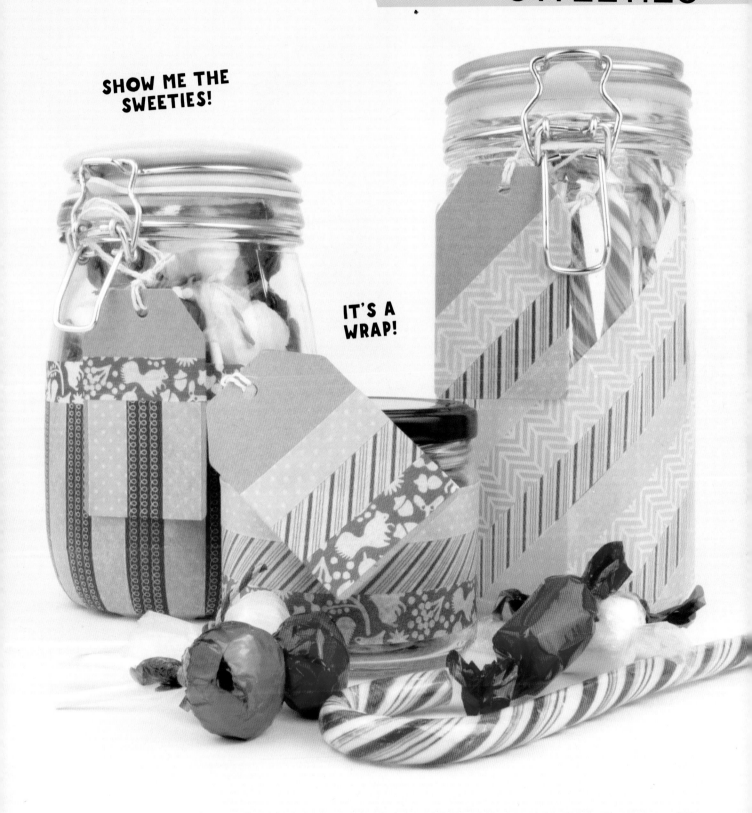

# TAPE-TASTIC SWEETIES

SHOW ME THE SWEETIES!

IT'S A WRAP!

# DOLL'S HOUSE
# BOOKCASE

MAKE A SHELF
A HOME!

**3.** Now arrange the pictures in each room and glue them inside. Finish off each room with some doll's furniture and dolls (if you have them).

**2.** Decide which rooms you want in your doll's house, then cut out pictures of furniture and furnishings from the magazines.

**1.** Cut out pieces of patterned paper, the same size as the back of each shelf in your bookcase, for the wallpaper. Then glue them in place.

## MATERIALS
old bookcase, home and furniture magazines, patterned paper, scissors, glue stick

# ARM-KNITTED SNOOD

WONDERFULLY
WOOLLY!

## MATERIALS
balls of wool x 4,
large needle

### 1.
Take a strand from each ball of wool
and line up the ends, as shown.

### 2.
Keeping hold of the yarn, measure
out six arm's-lengths of wool.

### 3.
Tie a slip knot near the end, leaving
the six arm's lengths as a tail.
Make sure you keep the four strands
of wool grouped together.

### 4.
Slide the knot onto your right wrist.

### 5.
In your left hand, hold the four
strands of working wool (the wool still
attached to the ball), then loop them
around your thumb and across your
palm. Hold the end of the wool, or the
tail, between two fingers, as shown.

tail

working wool

### 6.
Slide your right hand under the
working wool (stretched taut by your
thumb), then grab the tail (being
held by your fingers).

← tail

working
wool →

working
wool

← tail

### 7.
Pull the tail through the loop that
you have just created, but not
all the way.

27

**working wool**

**tail**

**working wool**

**tail**

**8.**
Pull the tail until you have a loop large enough to fit around your right wrist.

**9.**
Slide the loop onto your right wrist and tighten. This is called casting on.

**working wool**

**10.**
Repeat steps 5 to 9 ten more times, to make 11 casting-on stitches total. Now you are ready to start knitting. Let go of the tail, as you will only be using the working wool.

**11.**
Hold the working wool in your left hand.

**working wool**

**12.**
Use your left hand to pull a stitch off your right hand. At the same time, pull the working wool through the stitch with your right hand.

**working wool**

**13.**
Slide the loop (created by the working wool) onto your left wrist.

**14.**
Repeat steps 12 to 13 until all of the stitches have been transferred onto your left arm.

**15.**
Continue knitting, using alternate arms, until the knitted wool is 80 cm long.

**16.**
Now you're ready to cast off. First, knit two more stitches on your right arm.

second stitch

first stitch

**17.**
With your left hand, pull the first stitch on your right arm over the second stitch, then slide the stitch off your right hand, casting it off. Now pull the wool tight.

**18.**
Knit another stitch on your right arm. Again, pull the first stitch over the second, then slide it off your right hand. Tighten the wool. Continue until you have completely cast off all the stitches.

**19.**
Cut the working wool one arm's length from your last stitch, creating a tail. To prevent the knitting from undoing, pull the tail through the last stitch and tighten.

**20.**
Thread all four strands of the tail through the eye of a large needle. Fold the knitting in half, lining up the ends, as shown.

**21.**
Stitch the ends of the scarf together using the needle and tail.

**22.**
Now split the four tails into two, and tie them together twice to form a double knot (see page 12 to find out how to do this).

**23.**
Hide the remaining bit of tail by weaving it through the knitting with your needle, and you're done!

# MATERIALS
long balloon, paper (A3 size), pin, sticky tack, paintbrush, bowl of confetti stars, bowl of ¾ white glue and ¼ water mix (as shown)

### 1.
Blow up the balloon and tie a knot in the end. Place two balls of sticky tack on each end of the balloon, then place it on the paper. This will stop the balloon from moving.

### 2.
Now brush the glue mixture evenly over the entire top half of the balloon.

### 3.
Sprinkle the confetti stars over the balloon, covering as much of the glue area as possible. Leave to dry.

### 4.
Shake the balloon until all the loose confetti falls onto the paper. Remove the sticky tack from the paper, then pour the loose confetti back into the bowl.

### 5.
Repeat steps 1 to 4 three more times, until the top of the balloon is covered with a thin layer of confetti stars.

### 6.
Finally, paint the confetti with a layer of the glue mixture and leave to dry.

### 7.
Turn the balloon over, then pop it with a pin. Remove the balloon. Cut around the jagged edge so that it is straight, and fill with pencils!

GIVE YOUR STATIONERY A STARRING ROLE!

STAR-MÂCHÉ PENCIL CASE

# GLITTER BUG MAGNETS

CAN I BUG YOU?
PLEEEASE?

## MATERIALS

white glue

glitter nail polish

clear glass stones

self-adhesive flexible foam magnets

googly eyes

Bug yourself with lists, notes, mementos or reminders with these fab forget-me-not fridge magnets. Make them super-sparkly to stand out on your fridge!

**1.** Paint the back of a clear stone with some glitter nail polish. Leave to dry.

**2.** Add a few more coats of polish to give an even colour. Allow time to dry between each coat.

**3.** Read the instructions for the sticky magnet, then attach it to the back of the stone.

**4.** Glue googly eyes to the front of the stone. Create more glitter bugs, then place them on the fridge!

33

# MATERIALS

double duvet cover,
bamboo canes x 5
(each 180 cm long),
bamboo canes x 4
(each 50 cm long),
twine, scissors

30 cm

**1.** Wrap some twine around the five longer canes (30 cm down from the top of the canes). Tie the twine in a double knot, then cut it off.

**2.** Open out two of the canes from the bottom end. Place a shorter length of bamboo between them, then tie together using more twine, as shown, securing with double knots.

**3.** Repeat step 2 until all the shorter lengths of cane have been tied between the longer lengths, as shown.

**4.** Stand the frame up, arranging the canes into a tepee shape.

**5.** (a) Tie one corner of the duvet cover around the top of the tepee with a knot. (b) Repeat this step with the adjacent duvet cover corner.

**6.** Tie one remaining duvet cover corner around the bottom of each front bamboo cane to finish!

LET'S GO CAMPING!

DUVET DEN TEPEE

# MATERIALS
purple canvas fabric, coloured felt (black, white, yellow and pink), scissors, ruler, pencil, needle, thread, dried lentils

33 cm
14 cm
18 cm
7 cm

## 1.
Draw a cross 33 cm long x 14 cm wide onto the back of the canvas fabric. Draw lines to join the points to make a diamond. Now draw two triangles, 18 cm along each side and 7 cm at each base. Cut them out.

eyes (a)
mouth
tongue
hands
eyes (b)

## 2.
Sketch the eyes, mouth, tongue and hands onto the pieces of felt, as shown. Carefully cut these out too.

## 3.
Backstitch the black circles (a) onto the white ones (b) (for eyes), and the pink tongue in the black mouth. Turn the canvas fabric over to the front and stitch the eyes and mouth in the top half of the diamond.

## 4.
Place one yellow hand in the top half of the diamond. Now place the long side of a purple triangle on top, lining it up along the edge of the diamond. Backstitch along the edge so the hand is sandwiched between the two purple layers.

## 5.
Repeat step 4 on the other side of the diamond.

## 6.
Fold the bottom half of the diamond upwards so that the tips touch and the monster's face is on the inside.

## 7.
Now sew each open edge of the triangles to each open edge of the diamond, leaving a gap at the top.

## 8.
Turn the monster inside out, through the gap at the top, so its face is on the outside again. Fill your monster doorstop with dried lentils.

## 9.
Finish by folding in the top edges and sewing up the opening with a running stitch.

# DE-LIGHT-FUL CONFETTI CUPS

## MATERIALS

battery-powered fairy lights,
round tissue paper confetti,
paper cups, pencil, brush,
white glue, water

### 1.

Mix together ²/₃ white glue with
¹/₃ water in a bowl. Brush a small
amount of the mixture (about the size
of a confetti piece) onto a cup.

### 2.

Stick a single piece of confetti
onto the glue area, as shown.

FAIRY FABULOUS FOR PARTIES!

**3.**
Repeat steps 1 and 2, adding more confetti pieces to the cup. Try overlapping some.

**4.**
Turn the cup upside down and, using a sharp pencil, pierce a small hole in the base of the cup.

**5.**
Thread one fairy light through the hole in the cup. Repeat steps 1 to 4 until you have enough cups for all the lights.

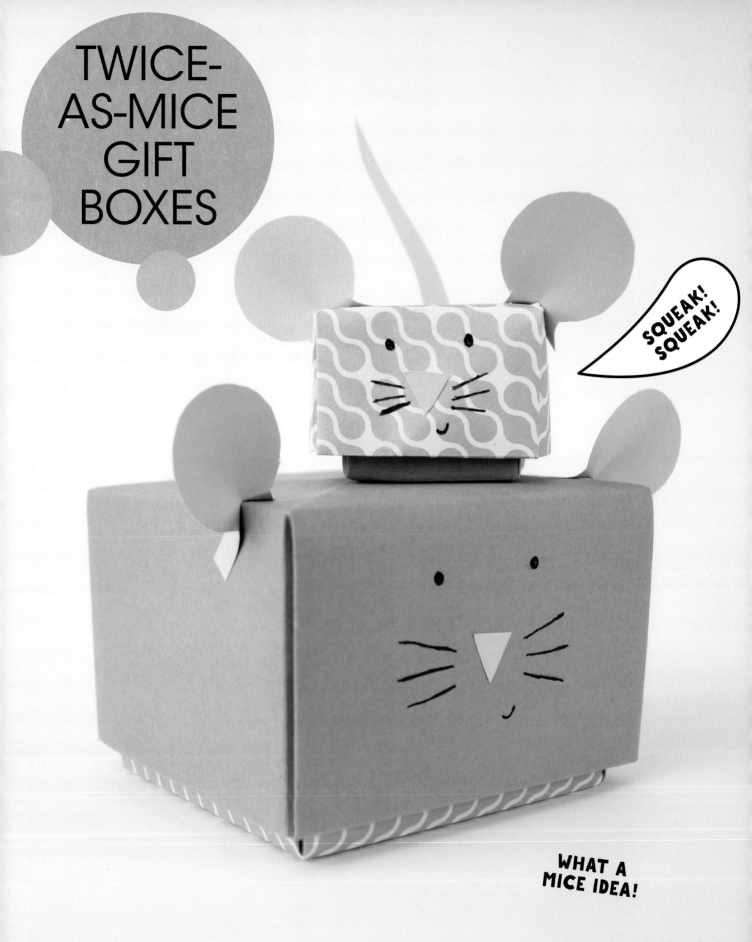

# TWICE-AS-MICE GIFT BOXES

SQUEAK! SQUEAK!

WHAT A MICE IDEA!

## MATERIALS

patterned paper x 4
(30 cm x 30 cm x 2, 15 cm x 15 cm x 2),
pink paper, ruler, scissors, pencil,
glue stick, black pen

**1.**
Use a 30 cm x 30 cm piece of paper
to create the base of your large box.

**2.**
Fold the paper in half, then unfold it.

**3.**
Fold the paper in half the other way,
and unfold.

**4.**
Turn the paper over onto the other
side. Fold one corner up into the
middle of the crease lines created in
steps 2 and 3.

**5.**
Repeat step 4 until all four corners
have been folded into the centre.

**6.**
Using your ruler, fold the right-hand
side towards the centre (6.5 cm in
from the edge), then unfold.

**7.**
Repeat step 6 for the left-hand,
bottom and top sides.

6.5 cm

41

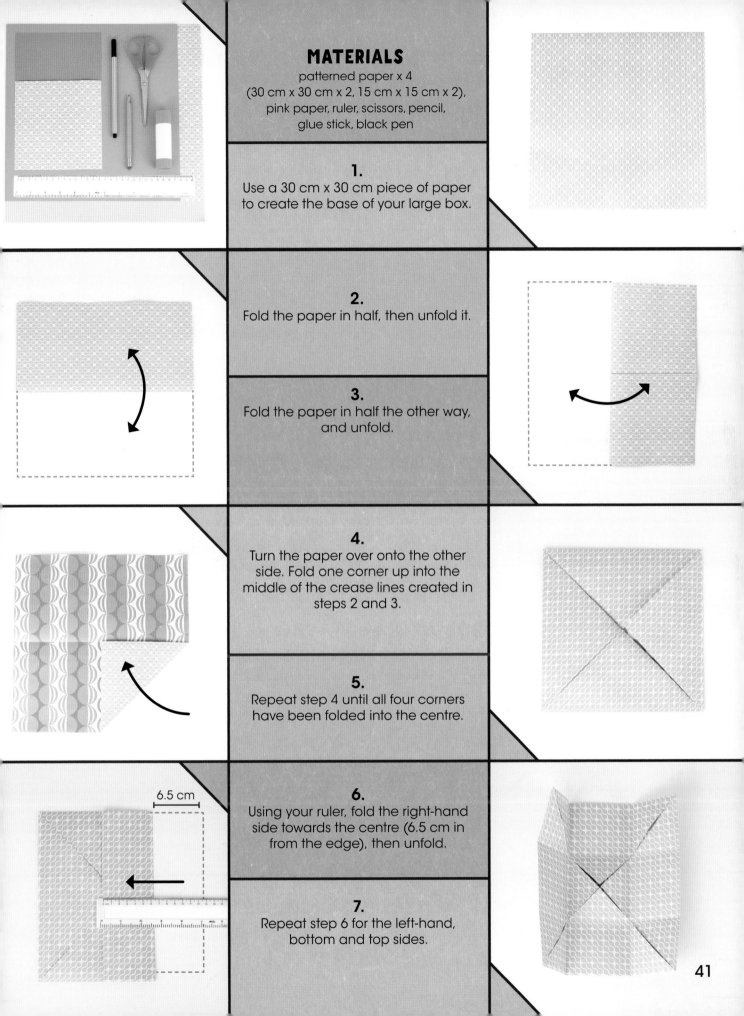

**8.**
Unfold the top triangle, as shown.

**9.**
Bring point 1 up and across, folding the crease in, as shown.

**10.**
Continue to bring point 1 up and across, folding the paper along the crease, as shown.

**11.**
Repeat steps 9 and 10 for point 2 on the left-hand side.

**12.**
Fold the top triangle and rectangle down into the centre of the box, as shown. This will complete three of your box sides.

**13.**
Repeat steps 8 to 12 for the unfolded box side.

**14.**
Repeat steps 2 to 13 with the same-sized square paper to make the lid. When you reach steps 6 and 7, only fold the edges in from 6 cm, so the base will fit inside the lid.

**15.**
To create the base of the smaller box, repeat steps 2 to 13 on one of the 15 cm x 15 cm pieces of paper. In steps 6 and 7, fold the edges in from 3.5 cm.

2 •      • 1

• 1

unfolded box side

• 2

**16.**
Repeat steps 2 to 13 with the same-sized paper to make the lid of the small box. In steps 6 and 7, only fold the edges in from 3 cm.

**17.**
To turn your boxes into mice, draw two tails and two triangular noses on the pink paper. Use the lid of the glue stick to create four circular ears. Add a rectangular tab to each ear.

**18.**
Carefully cut out all the pieces.

**19.**
Snip a slot in each of the rectangular tabs, as shown. These will help to fix the ears to the boxes in step 21.

**20.**
Turn the lid of the large box over and glue one of the tails inside the inner edge. Gently bend the tail a little so it sticks out of the lid.

**21.**
Glue a nose in the middle of the lid on the opposite side to the tail. Then dab some glue on an ear tab. Stick one side of the slot on the top of the lid, and the other down its side. Repeat with the other ear.

**22.**
Finish off the large box by drawing some whiskers, eyes and a mouth with the black pen.

**23.**
Repeat steps 20 to 22 on the small box to finish. Squeak!

## MATERIALS
plain tote bag, blue and yellow embroidery thread, needle, ruler, pencil, scissors

**1.**
With your pencil and ruler, lightly draw a grid across the front of the tote bag. Space the vertical lines 3 cm apart, and the horizontal lines 1.5 cm apart.

**2.**
Start from the top left corner and place four dots where one horizontal line meets a vertical line. Draw the dots on the lines, evenly spaced around the cross. Continue across the bag in a similar pattern as shown.

**3.**
First, sew on some yellow crosses. Start from inside the bag, feeding the needle through a dot at the bottom of a cross and over into the dot opposite.

**4.**
Now feed the needle through the dot at the side, and over into the dot opposite. Pull the thread tightly to form a cross.

**5.**
Tie the thread ends together in a double knot on the inside of the bag and trim with your scissors. Repeat steps 3 and 4 in a few different places on the bag.

**6.**
For the blue stitches, start from the bottom left inside the bag, feeding the needle through a dot at the bottom of the cross, and over into the dot opposite. Then repeat for the cross above, continuing to form vertical blue lines up and down the bag.

**7.**
Now work your way back across the bag, sewing horizontal blue lines through the vertical lines to finish. Tie a double knot at the end!

# SUPER-STITCH TOTE BAG

# PEASY PRINT GIFT WRAP

Who needs to buy wrapping paper when you can make your own? From buttons to bubble wrap, and paintbrushes to potatoes, be inspired to create brilliant prints using everyday objects found around the home.

Patterned buttons make fab stampers. Glue them to something sturdy (like cork stoppers) to prevent your fingers from getting messy!

Have fun with easy-peasy potato prints. Try hearts, stars and smiley faces, or opt for a simple semicircle pattern!

For instant printing, use the end of a toilet roll and create some seriously cool circles!

Stencils make great patterns, like this raindrop effect. Just cut out your design from card, then paint over the top!

Raid your pencil case and create a polka-dot pattern using the end of a pencil (or pen) dipped in an ink pad.

For a more detailed print, stamp two colours at the same time from a piece of shaped sponge. Once dry, add any finer details (like the seeds in this watermelon) using more paint and a brush!

Brush poster paint over bubble wrap for a brilliant bubbly design!

47

BUZZ!

WHAT
BEE-UTIFUL
FLOWERS!

# NIFTY
# NAIL
# POLISH
# FLOWERS

# MATERIALS
coloured nail polish, jewellery wire,
jewellery pliers (with cutter), thin metal rod or
wooden skewer, jar, pen

## 1.
Cut the jewellery wire to 40 cm long, then bend
the middle part of the wire around the barrel
of a pen using the pliers. Now rotate the pen
so that the wire becomes twisted together
beneath the loop on the pen. Slide the wire
loop off the pen.

## 2.
Next, wrap one end of the wire around the
pen to create another loop next to the first
one. Feed the same end of the wire through
the centre of the first loop, to join them
together. Then repeat to create a third loop
with the other end of the wire.

## 3.
As the loops start to look like flower petals,
twist both ends of the wire near the centre, to
tie them all together.

## 4.
Repeat steps 2 and 3 to form two more petals.
You may need to move the position of the first
three petals to make room.

## 5.
Now place the flower on the metal rod or
wooden skewer, as shown. Take one end of
the wire and wrap it tightly around the skewer.
Do the same with the other end of the wire,
but twist it around the skewer in the opposite
direction.

## 6.
To create a leaf, cut the wire to 10 cm long, then
bend the middle around the pen using the pliers.
Rotate the pen so that the wire twists together
beneath the loop on the pen. Slide the loop off
the pen, then pinch it into a leaf shape. Create
more leaves in the same way!

## 7.
Pour the nail polish into a jar. Dip the petals
and leaves into the polish until fully coated.
Leave to dry between each coat. Finally, twist
the leaves around the skewers and place your
flowers in a vase or bottle to finish.

# SWEET DOUGHNUT CUSHIONS

## MATERIALS

felt (beige, pink, dark brown and white),
paper plate x 2, pencil, scissors, needle, thread,
embroidery thread (yellow, pink, blue and green),
toy stuffing

**1.** First fold a paper plate in half. Then draw a semicircle inside it, as shown.

**2.** Carefully cut along the line and unfold the plate to reveal a hole in the middle.

**3.** Repeat steps 1 and 2 on another paper plate. Then draw two squiggly circles, as shown.

**4.** Cut along each line to make a ring. These are now the templates for your doughnut cushions.

**5.** For the main doughnut shape, draw around the circular plate onto two pieces of beige felt.

**6.** Trace the squiggly shape onto one of the other felt colours. This will be the icing.

**7.** Carefully cut out all of the pieces, as shown.

**8.** Create the look of sprinkles by sewing large stitches of different colours all over the felt icing.

**9.** Now sew the felt icing onto one of the beige circles. Stitch all around both edges of the icing.

**10.** Keep the other beige circle plain (as this will be the bottom of the doughnut ring).

**11.** Pin the two beige rings together, with the icing on the inside.

**12.** Stitch the circles together, going all around the outer edges.

**13.** Turn out the doughnut so the icing is now on the outside, as shown.

**14.** Stitch ¾ of the way around the inner edges of the rings, leaving an opening for the stuffing.

**15.** Feed the stuffing through the hole until the doughnut shape is completely full.

**16.** Sew the opening up to finish. Make more doughnut ring cushions with different-coloured felt icing. Delicious!

# SELFIE POSING PROPS

## MATERIALS

coloured card, wooden skewers,
pencil, scissors, glue gun*

* Ask an adult to use the glue gun in step 3!

1. Draw or trace some fun moustaches, beards, hats, glasses, ties or whatever you wish onto the back of different pieces of coloured card.

2. Carefully cut out all of the shapes.

3. Dab some glue in one corner of each piece using the glue gun.*

    * Ask an adult to do this!

4. Press a skewer firmly onto the glue.

**GRAB A PROP AND STRIKE A POSE!**

MY FAMILY

MY SISTER
AND ME

DAD

MUM AND ME

Show off fabulous family photos with this washi tape family tree. Create new branches, add more pictures and update any old ones as you go!*

## MATERIALS
brown, green (a few shades and patterns), yellow, orange and red rolls of washi tape, scissors

**1.** Clean a big wall space area, then run strips of brown and yellow washi tape from the floor upwards to make the tree trunk (150 cm long). The trunk should be wider at the bottom and taper to a point at the top.

**2.** For the branches, run different lengths of tape at angles from the trunk, as shown. Again, make the branches wider at the bottom and narrower near the top. Add smaller lengths of brown tape for the twigs.

**3.** To make a leaf shape, first cut out some green tape (17 cm long) for the stem, then stick it on the wall near the branches. Now add four smaller lengths of tape for the veins and place on the stem, as shown.

**4.** Use another shade of green for the outer edges of the leaf. Tape four strips around the stem and the veins to form a diamond. Repeat steps 3 and 4 to make more leaves in different shades and colours.

**5.** To make each flower, first cut four strips of orange washi tape for the petals. Keep the strips the same length (8 cm each), then snip the ends to form triangular tips.

**6.** Stick one orange strip on the wall, then add another on top to form a cross. Add the other two strips, as shown, and cut out a small yellow square for the middle of the flower. Repeat steps 5 and 6 to make more flowers. Now tape your photos to the wall!

# MATERIALS

drinking straws x 5, scissors, string

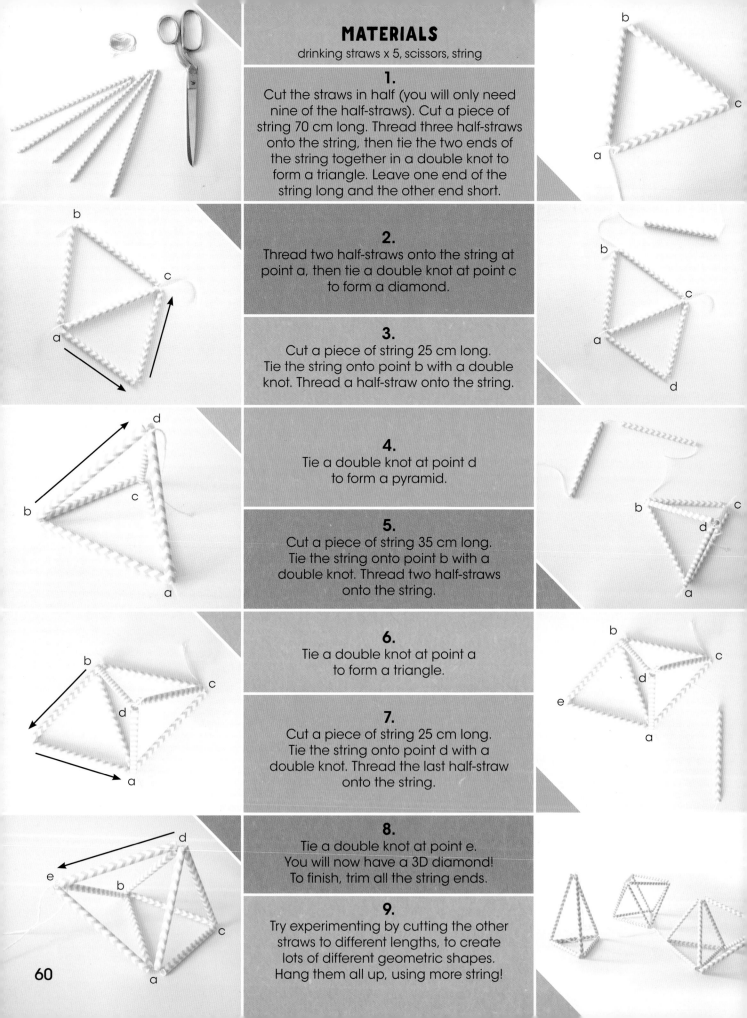

**1.**
Cut the straws in half (you will only need nine of the half-straws). Cut a piece of string 70 cm long. Thread three half-straws onto the string, then tie the two ends of the string together in a double knot to form a triangle. Leave one end of the string long and the other end short.

**2.**
Thread two half-straws onto the string at point a, then tie a double knot at point c to form a diamond.

**3.**
Cut a piece of string 25 cm long. Tie the string onto point b with a double knot. Thread a half-straw onto the string.

**4.**
Tie a double knot at point d to form a pyramid.

**5.**
Cut a piece of string 35 cm long. Tie the string onto point b with a double knot. Thread two half-straws onto the string.

**6.**
Tie a double knot at point a to form a triangle.

**7.**
Cut a piece of string 25 cm long. Tie the string onto point d with a double knot. Thread the last half-straw onto the string.

**8.**
Tie a double knot at point e. You will now have a 3D diamond! To finish, trim all the string ends.

**9.**
Try experimenting by cutting the other straws to different lengths, to create lots of different geometric shapes. Hang them all up, using more string!

60

# STRAW-SOME SHAPES

61

Upcycle an old jar into a brightly coloured vase with this easy-peasy craft. Try adding more amazing creations to your budding collection with different-shaped jars (or bottles) and colours.

poster paints     glass jar (or bottle)

funnel

MATERIALS

**1.**
Place the funnel on the top of a clean, dry jar (or bottle).*

* Ask an adult to clean the jar in a dishwasher or with hot water and washing-up liquid.

**2.**
Pour some poster paint into the bottom of the jar through the funnel.

**3.**
Tip the jar on its side and let the paint flow down the side of the jar. Keep turning the jar around for an even coat of paint along the sides.

**4.**
Continue to rotate the sides of the jar until the paint is right up to the rim of the jar. Then leave to dry.

GO COLOUR CRAZY!

# POUR-IN PAINT VASES

# PAPER-SHAPER CHAIN BELT

A FABULOUS
WAIST OF
PAPER!

64

## MATERIALS

patterned paper x 15,
self-adhesive hook-and-loop
fastener (15 cm long),
bulldog clips x 2,
white glue,
scissors

Turn patterned paper into a brilliant belt! Fold and link lots of pieces of paper together to make your very own paper-trail accessory.

**1.** First measure your waist, then add an extra 11 cm. This will be the length of your paper chain. Now cut the paper into lots of strips, each one measuring 5 cm x 15 cm.

**2.** First, fold each strip in half lengthwise to mark the centre. Unfold and then fold each strip lengthwise twice, bringing each edge towards the centre.

**3.** Now fold along the centre line, so the folded edges from step 2 are on the inside.

**4.** Now fold the strip in half widthwise to mark the centre. Unfold and then fold each strip widthwise twice, bringing each edge towards the centre.

65

**5.** Then fold along the centre line, so the folded edges from step 4 are on the inside.

**6.** Pinch the two ends together.

**7.** Repeat steps 1 to 6 until you have lots of folded pieces. Now you're ready to get connecting.

**8.** Insert the ends of one piece though the folds of another.

**9.** Push the inserted piece all the way through, as shown.

**10.** Insert another piece of folded paper through the last piece added.

**11.** Your paper chain should look like this.

**12.** Continue adding the folded paper, one at a time, until the belt has reached the size needed.

**13.** Glue together the open ends (at either end of the belt).

**14.** Attach bulldog clips over each end, and allow plenty of time to dry.

**15.** Cut the hook-and-loop fastener into three sections, the same size as the last three pieces of paper on the belt. Glue the loop sides to one end.

**16.** To finish, stick the hook sides on the last three pieces of paper at the other end of the belt!

# MATERIALS

empty cotton reels x 3, adhesive paper, wooden skewer, pencil, black pen, coloured pens, white glue, scissors, tape measure

## 1.

Measure between the outer rims of a reel, from top to bottom. Then measure the circumference, as shown.

## 2.

For one spinner, cut out three pieces of adhesive paper, all the same height and circumference as the reel. Sketch three different characters on each strip, drawing their heads on one strip, bodies on the second and legs and feet on the third. Colour in the characters, then go over the lines with a black pen.

## 3.

Remove the backing from the strips and wrap each one around a reel.

## 4.

On another piece of adhesive paper, draw around the base of a reel to create a circle. Cut out the circle.

## 5.

Glue the circle at the bottom of the third reel (the one with the legs and feet).

## 6.

Cut the skewer so that it is 1 cm taller than the three reels stacked on top of each other. Place the shortened skewer in the centre of the third reel. Add a good amount of glue to the hole, making sure that the skewer is standing up straight. Leave to dry.

## 7.

Add the other two reels to the skewer, then turn them to change outfits and hairstyles. You've made a friend!

68

# DINO-MITE CHESS GAME

## MATERIALS

plastic dinosaur models x 32 (see 'Key' for details),
blue card (40 cm x 40 cm), orange card (40 cm x 20 cm),
glue stick, paintbrush, yellow and red acrylic paint

**1.** Divide the dinos into two equal sets, with the same number of species in each.

**2.** Paint one set yellow and the other red. Leave to dry between each coat (you may need up to three).

**3.** Draw 32 squares (each 5 cm x 5 cm) onto the orange card, then cut them out.

**4.** Glue the orange squares onto the blue card in a chequerboard pattern.

**5.** Look at the 'Key' below and get ready to play dino chess!

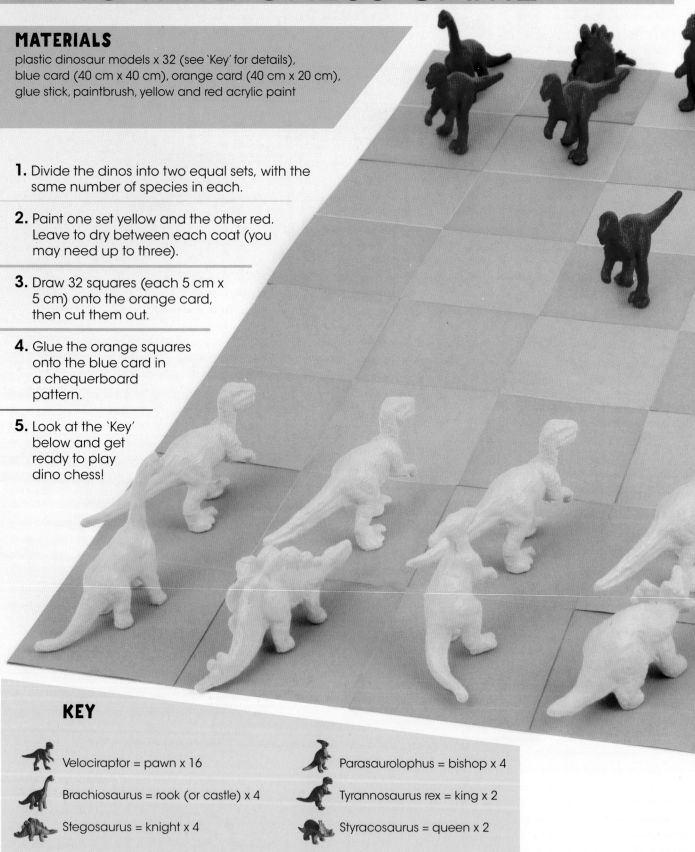

## KEY

Velociraptor = pawn x 16

Brachiosaurus = rook (or castle) x 4

Stegosaurus = knight x 4

Parasaurolophus = bishop x 4

Tyrannosaurus rex = king x 2

Styracosaurus = queen x 2

If you're not sure how to play chess, ask an adult to help you look up the rules online.

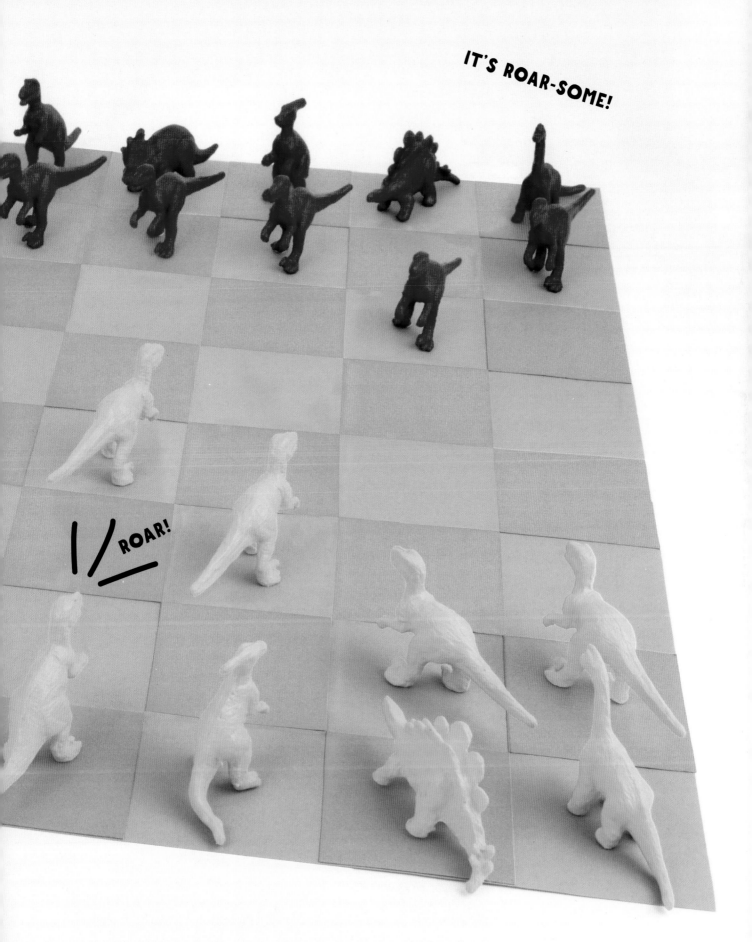

IT'S ROAR-SOME!

ROAR!

## MATERIALS

grid paper (or if making grid paper: white card, pencil, ruler), brown card, coloured embroidery threads, needle, awl, scissors, coloured pencils

### 1.

To make a template, use grid paper or create your own (draw 26 squares across and 24 squares down onto white card – each square to be ½ cm). Then sketch a cupcake onto the grid, colouring the squares as you go.

### 2.

Fold the brown card in half, then place the cupcake template in the centre. Use the awl to push holes through each corner of the coloured squares, making sure you only go through the front of the card (and not the back too).

### 3.

Continue until all of the holes have been made, revealing a cupcake shape, as shown.

### 4.

Using your template as a guide, start sewing in the cherry details using a cross-stitch. To do this, bring your needle and thread up and over two diagonal holes, as shown.

### 5.

Make another diagonal stitch over the top to form a cross, as shown. This is called a cross-stitch!

### 6.

Continue adding the decorative details (like the sprinkles) with cross-stitches.

### 7.

To finish, cross-stitch the main bit of the cake, such as the icing and cake wrapper. Yum!

72

CAKE IT ALL
THE WAY!

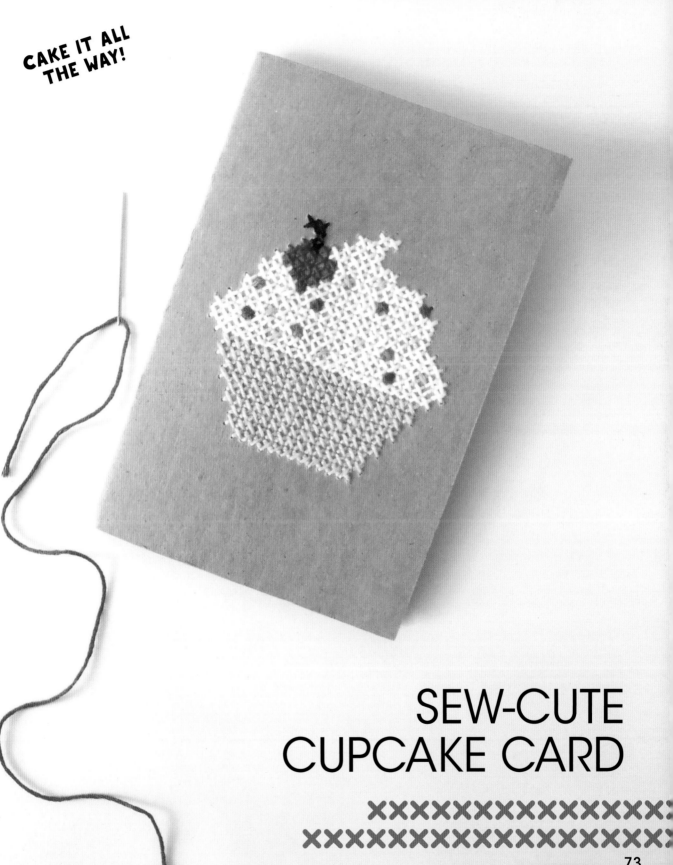

# SEW-CUTE
# CUPCAKE CARD

A lava lamp is a light filled with a coloured oily mixture. As the mixture moves up and down, it makes a blobby shape and pattern. Create a similar lava lamp effect with this simple craft!

**MATERIALS**
water, food colouring, fizzy (dissolving) tablet*, empty glass bottle or jar, vegetable oil

* Ask an adult to help when using the tablet.

**1.**
Clean the glass bottle (or jar), then fill it ¼ full of water.*

* Ask an adult to clean the bottle (or jar) in a dishwasher or with hot water and washing-up liquid.

**2.**
Now pour the oil right up to the neck of the bottle, as shown.

**3.**
Add a few drops of food colouring, then watch it sink through the oil and mix with the water.

**4.**
Add a piece of the fizzy tablet to the bottle.* The water will mix with the oil, creating a lava-lamp-like display. Each time the bubbling stops, add another piece of tablet and watch it again!

* Ask an adult to do this!

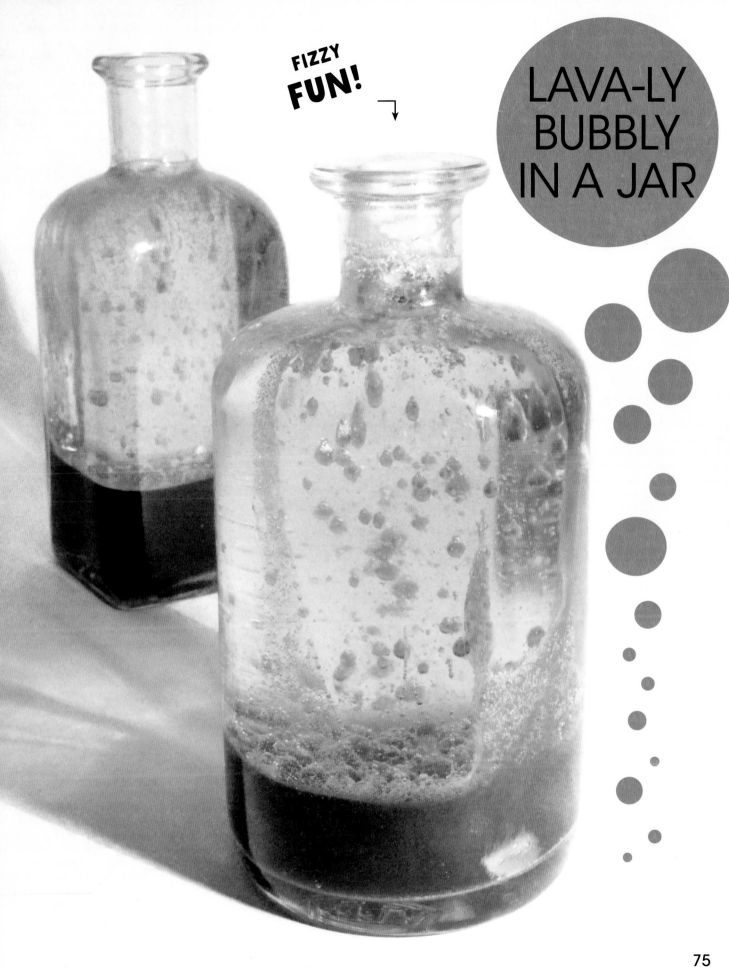

FIZZY **FUN!**

LAVA-LY BUBBLY IN A JAR

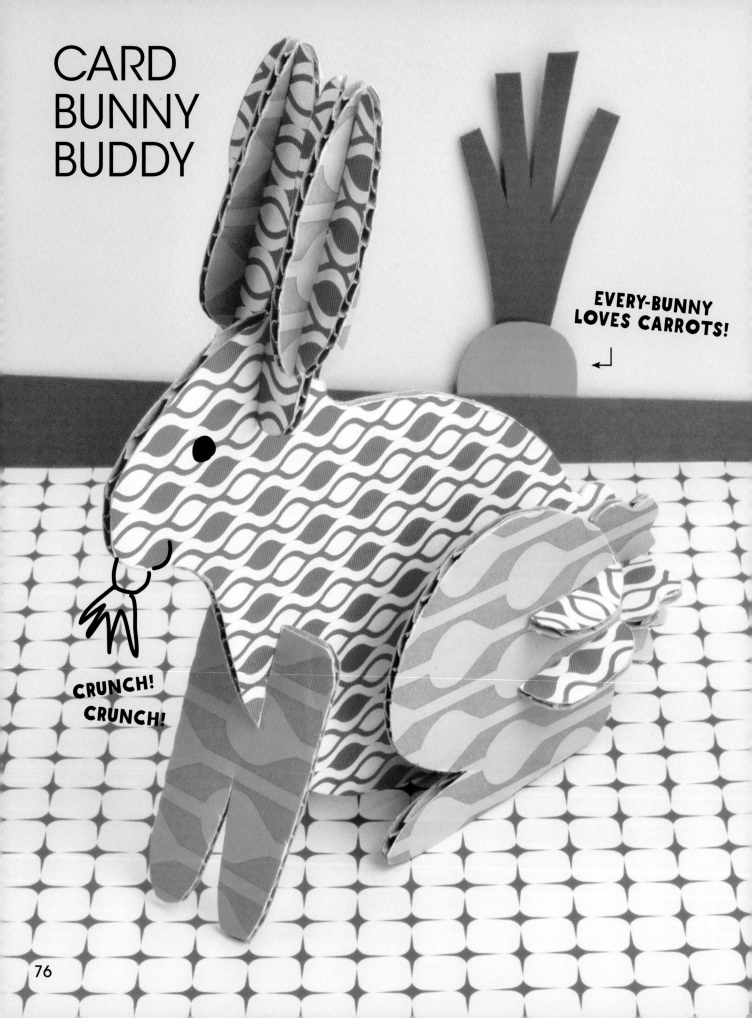

# CARD
# BUNNY
# BUDDY

EVERY-BUNNY
LOVES CARROTS!

CRUNCH!
CRUNCH!

## MATERIALS

corrugated card (A4 size),
patterned paper x 2 (A4 size),
tracing paper (A4 size),
HB pencil,
soft pencil,
glue stick,
scissors,
bunny template (see page 79)

**1.** Place the tracing paper onto the bunny template, then carefully draw over the outlines using a soft pencil.

**2.** Turn the tracing paper over and place it onto a sheet of patterned paper. Now go over the outlines with a HB pencil, to transfer them onto the patterned paper.

**3.** Glue the patterned paper onto the card, then glue another sheet of patterned paper to the other side of the card.

**4.** Cut out all of the bunny pieces, taking care to follow the pencil lines closely so the pieces will easily slot together.

**5.** Look at the bunny template as you do the next steps. First find the tail pieces, then fold *Tail 2* and *Tail 3* along the dashed lines to form right angles.

**6.** Slide *Tail 2* and *Tail 3* (slots b and c) into *Tail 1* (slot a), to make a 3D bunny tail.

77

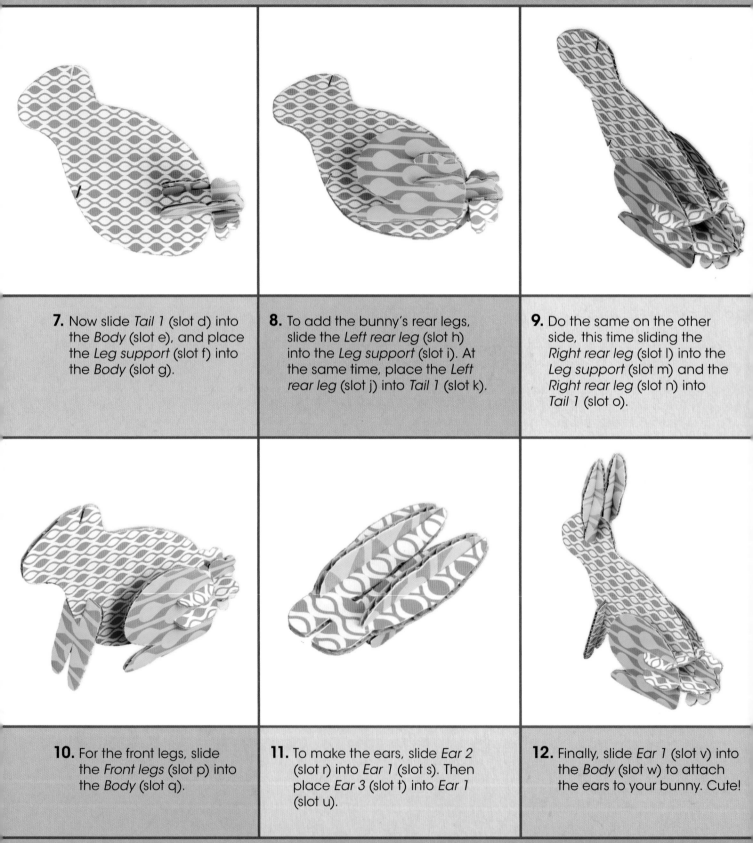

**7.** Now slide *Tail 1* (slot d) into the *Body* (slot e), and place the *Leg support* (slot f) into the *Body* (slot g).

**8.** To add the bunny's rear legs, slide the *Left rear leg* (slot h) into the *Leg support* (slot i). At the same time, place the *Left rear leg* (slot j) into *Tail 1* (slot k).

**9.** Do the same on the other side, this time sliding the *Right rear leg* (slot l) into the *Leg support* (slot m) and the *Right rear leg* (slot n) into *Tail 1* (slot o).

**10.** For the front legs, slide the *Front legs* (slot p) into the *Body* (slot q).

**11.** To make the ears, slide *Ear 2* (slot r) into *Ear 1* (slot s). Then place *Ear 3* (slot t) into *Ear 1* (slot u).

**12.** Finally, slide *Ear 1* (slot v) into the *Body* (slot w) to attach the ears to your bunny. Cute!

# BUNNY TEMPLATE

Body

w

Tail 1

k

a          d

o

q

Fold along
the dashed
line to form a
right angle.

b

Tail 2

Tail 3

c

g

e

Left rear leg          h

j

Leg support

m     f     i

s          u

Ear 1

v

Front legs

p

Ear 2

r

Ear 3

t

l          Right rear leg

n

# MATERIALS
pencil, card, white glue, ruler, scissors, wool, masking tape

## 1.
Cut out a strip of card, 10 cm x 3 cm (or 8 cm x 2 cm for smaller pom-poms). Cut a piece of wool 10 cm long and tape it to the card, as shown. Now start wrapping the wool around the card.

## 2.
Make sure the card is evenly wrapped and the wool is not pulled too tight. When you've covered most of the card, tuck the last bit of wool inside the wrapping and carefully remove the masking tape.

## 3.
Slide the wrapped wool off the card, but keep the separate piece of wool running through the middle. Tie the piece of wool into a double knot so that the wound wool bunches into a ball.

## 4.
Using your scissors, carefully cut through all the loops of wool until you have a rough circular pom-pom shape.

## 5.
Trim the edges to neaten up your pom-pom shape. Then repeat the steps until you have lots of different-sized and -coloured pom-poms.

## 6.
Using a ruler and pencil, draw a large letter onto another piece of card, 12 cm x 7 cm. Then cut it out.

## 7.
Finally, cover the letter with glue and stick the pom-poms closely together onto the card. Show the world your woolly letter!

# FANT-AZTEC LAMPSHADE

The Aztec people were known for creating beautiful art. Brighten up your room with a lampshade inspired by Aztec patterns. For a modern twist, go for super-bright neon colours!

## MATERIALS
neon highlighter pens,
black marker pen,
plain paper lampshade

**1.**
With the marker pen, draw lines all around the lampshade.

**2.**
Now add vertical lines up the sides of the lampshade, crossing over the horizontal lines to form sections.

**3.**
Doodle different patterns in each section. Try spots, stripes, zigzags or diamonds for Aztec-inspired designs.

**4.**
Finally, colour each pattern using the neon highligher pens. Leave some sections or patterns free from colour for an even more dazzling effect.

LIGHT UP YOUR DOODLES!

# WASH BAG
# BEASTIE

## MATERIALS

old bath towel,
felt (white, blue, orange),
self-adhesive hook-and-loop fasteners,
ruler,
pencil,
compass,
black marker pen,
scissors,
needle,
thread,
sewing machine (optional)

— folded edge

**1.**
Fold the bath towel in half, then use a ruler to measure 60 cm from the folded edge. Use the ruler and marker pen to draw a guide line on the towel.

**2.**
Now measure 40 cm from the left edge of the towel. Carefully cut along the guide lines until you have a smaller rectangle.

40 cm

60 cm

**3.**
Draw two curved edges at the fold, then carefully cut off the corners.

**4.**
To create the monster's eyes, use the compass to draw two 9-cm circles on the blue felt. Then draw two 11-cm circles on the white felt. Cut out the circles.

85

**5.**
Now sew the blue circles onto the white circles,

**6.**
Then sew the eyes onto the towel. Make sure only to sew through the top layer of the towel.

2 cm

**7.**
With the marker pen, draw a large, fun-shaped mouth, making it big enough for your laundry to fit through. Then unfold the towel and cut out the mouth, leaving a 2-cm gap between the pen line and the section to cut out, as shown.

**8.**
Fold the edge back around the mouth, until the pen line is no longer visible, then sew around the mouth, either using the sewing machine or by hand.

**9.**
Your monster's mouth should look a bit like the picture on the left.

**10.**
Place the white felt inside the mouth, then draw on some teeth with a pencil.

**11.**
Cut along the pencil marks, leaving a 2-cm gap at the top.

**12.**
Sew the teeth inside the mouth, either using the sewing machine or by hand. Now turn the towel inside out, with the seams showing.

**13.**
Stitch around the three (unfolded) sides of the towel. Then pull the towel back through the monster's mouth so the seams are on the inside again.

**14.**
Cut out a pair of feet and arms from the yellow felt.

**15.**
Cut out two pieces from the hook-and-loop fastener. Separate the hook from the loop, then stitch them on opposite sides of the monster's hand. Repeat on the other hand.

**16.**
Sew the arms and feet to the back of the towel. Now place the hands over a rail and fold the fingers down until the hook-and-loop fasteners stick together. Grrrrreat!

2 cm

Keep your secrets under wraps in this pretty patterned diary. Just grab some ribbon and glue, and get weaving!

**MATERIALS**
plain diary
(or notebook),
blue ribbon,
silver ribbon,
all-purpose glue,
scissors
↵

**1.**
Measure the width of the front cover. Cut the silver ribbon into strips, each 2 cm longer than this measurement. Now measure the length of the front cover. Cut the blue ribbon into strips, each 2 cm longer than this measurement.

**2.**
Lay the ribbon strips side by side on the front cover to check that you have enough. Now glue one side of each silver strip (1 cm in from the edge) down the length of the inside cover.

**3.**
Repeat until all the silver ribbon has been glued to the top of the inside cover, then leave to dry. Now add some glue to the spine. Pull each strip of silver ribbon across the front of the book, gluing in place on the spine. Once the glue has dried, trim any excess length of ribbon.

**4.**
Now glue one side of each blue strip (1 cm in from the edge) along the width of the inside cover, as shown. Then leave to dry.

**5.**
Weave the blue ribbon in and out of the silver ribbon, making any pattern you choose.

**6.**
Once you have completed your pattern, glue the blue ribbon to the bottom of the inside cover to finish. Why not create a smaller ribbon weave notebook to match?

# RIBBON
# WEAVE
# DIARY

SHH!
TOP SECRET!

## MATERIALS
pair of socks, scissors, needle, thread, buttons x 2, felt, black marker pen

phone inside

### 1.
Turn one sock inside out, then slide your phone inside, just above the ankle. Mark a line 1 cm below where your phone sits.

### 2.
Remove the phone, then sew the two layers of the sock together, following the mark made in step 1.

### 3.
Now trim off the sock foot, 1 cm below the stitched line.

### 4.
Use the stitched sock as a guide for the other sock, but make it 2 cm shorter. Turn the socks around the right way, so the stitching is on the inside.

### 5.
Sew a button on each side of the elastic area of the small, outer sock. Push the larger sock inside the smaller one.

### 6.
Cut a strip of felt long enough to stretch from one button to the other, going over the top of both socks. Measure carefully and snip a slot at each end of the felt, to make buttonholes.

### 7.
Slide both buttons through the buttonholes, making sure the felt wraps over the top of your cosy phone case.

ROCK YOUR
SOCKS OFF!

Keep fidgeting fingers busy with these cute sensory balls. Give each character a different expression to match how you feel!

**1.** Partially fill the sandwich bag with flour, making sure it's not too big to hold in your hand. Tie a double knot at the top, letting out air as you go. Cut the bag above the knot.

**2.** Then snip the narrow end or 'neck' off the white balloon. Leave ½ cm of the 'neck' on the wider section, as shown.

**3.** Push the bag of flour inside the white balloon, knotted end first. Squash the balloon into a round ball.

**4.** Flatten the red balloon, then snip it twice to create a hole near the wider end of the balloon. This will be an eye.

**5.** Repeat step 4 to snip another hole for the other eye. When flattened, the holes in the balloon should look quite small. Repeat step 2, then stretch the red balloon over the white ball.

**6.** The eye holes should now be bigger. Draw pupils, then add eyebrows and a mouth. Repeat steps 1 to 5 to create more emoji characters. Make the eye holes bigger or smaller for different expressions.

**MATERIALS**

flour,
sandwich bag,
scissors,
spoon,
white balloon,
...ed balloon,
...ker pen

...r jar),

...iling water

1. Place the craft sticks in a pan of boiling water for 30 minutes. Carefully remove the sticks from the pan, then leave to cool (but not dry out) before the next step.*

* Ask an adult to do all of this for you.

2. The sticks should now be soft enough to bend into curves. Do this slowly, so the sticks don't snap.

3. Place each curved stick into the base of a small cup and leave overnight to dry. This will help to form a cuff shape.

4. Add some glue to the inside of each curved stick (arm cuff). Tightly wrap some thread around the cuff, as shown. Start a little way in from one end of each cuff.

5. To change thread colours, snip off the previous thread, then add the new colour next to it, as shown. Finish a little way in from the end, then snip away any excess thread. Add more glue if necessary.

# STICK-ERRIFIC ARM CUFFS

**DROP THREAD GORGEOUS!**

# PICTURE HOLDERS

DON'T
LET
GO!

COO!
COO!

# MATERIALS

coloured paper,
patterned paper,
white card (A4 size),
tracing paper (A4 size),
pigeon templates (right),
scissors,
wooden pegs,
soft pencil,
HB pencil,
glue stick,
white glue,
string

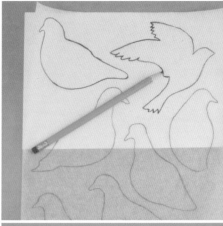

**1.** Cut a piece of white card in half, then glue a sheet of patterned paper to the back.

**2.** Place the tracing paper on the pigeon template, then carefully draw over the outlines using a soft pencil.

**3.** Turn the tracing paper over and place it on the plain side of the card. Now go over two of the pigeon outlines with a HB pencil, to transfer them onto the card.

**4.** Carefully cut out the pigeon shapes using your scissors.

**5.** Use white glue to attach each peg to the back of a pigeon shape. Leave the glue to dry. Repeat steps 1 to 5 to make more peg pigeons.

**6.** Hang up a line or two of twine along a wall.* Peg the pigeons on the twine, then add a gift card or picture beneath each one.

* Ask an adult for help!

# ZIP-MOUTH MONSTERS

ZIP
IT!

## MATERIALS

silicone cake moulds x 2
(each the same size),
zipper (same length as
circumference of
cake moulds),
craft foam,
black pen,
all-purpose glue,*
needle,
thread,
scissors

*Ask for an adult's help with the all-purpose glue in step 4!

**1.** Using a running stitch, sew one side of the zipper along the inside rim of a cake mould. Try to sew as close to the zipper as possible.

**2.** Unzip the zipper, then sew the unstitched side around the rim of the second cake mould. Place it on top of the other mould.

**3.** Draw eyes, eyebrows and a nose on your craft foam, then cut them out.

**4.** Glue the features onto the base of the upside down cake mould. Now create some more monster friends for your zip-mouth monster.

101

# WASHI TAPE MAKEOVERS

From single strips to diagonal stripes, let washi tape work its magic and give everyday items a new lease of life!

Jazz up boring bulldog clips with brightly coloured washi tape! Just cut them to size and stick them on. Simple!

Transform a cup into a pencil pot with a dazzling diagonal design.

Decorate pegs washi-tape style, then use them as note holders and picture hangers, or add magnets to the back and stick them on your fridge!

102

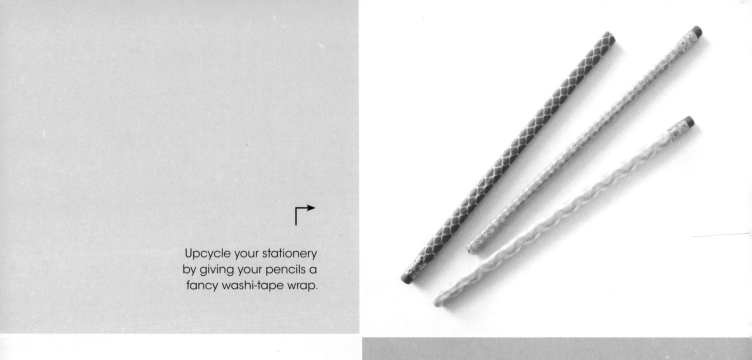

Upcycle your stationery by giving your pencils a fancy washi-tape wrap.

There's no need to fork out for new photo frames... Revamp yours with alternating strips of tape, like this!

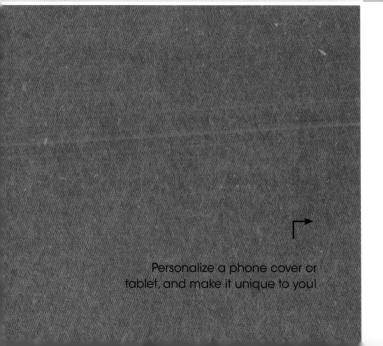

Personalize a phone cover or tablet, and make it unique to you!

# MATERIALS

yellow felt, cream felt, zipper
(same length as width of felt),
pencil, scissors, needle, pin, thread

## 1.

Fold the yellow felt in half and draw
a semicircle next to the open edge
(opposite the folded edge), the
same width as the zipper. Cut out
both layers of felt, so you end up
with two semicircles.

## 2.

Now draw around one of the
semicircles onto the cream felt. Draw
another semicircle inside it, making
it 1.5 cm smaller all around, then cut
out the smaller semicircle. Next, cut
out four triangles from more yellow felt.
These need to be small enough to fit
inside the cream felt.

## 3.

Sew the yellow triangles onto the
cream felt with a running stitch.

## 4.

Now sew the cream felt onto one of
the yellow semicircles. The felt should
start to look like a fruit segment.

## 5.

Sew both yellow semicircles on either
side of the zipper, leaving ½ cm
between the top edge of each piece
of felt and the teeth of the zipper,
as shown.

## 6.

Fold the fruit in half so that the
edges of the two semicircles line up.
Tuck in the excess zipper on each
side, and pin in place.

## 7.

Starting at the top left corner, next to
the zipper, stitch the felt all the way
around and back to the zipper on the
other side, making sure to sew in the
zipper ends. Remove all pins, then
make more fruity pouches!

MADE WITH
ZEST!

# MATERIALS

patterned paper and card (large enough to cover the tissue box)

number stamps (each 1 cm x 1 cm)

empty square-shaped tissue box

twine

white glue

beads

scissors

stamp pad

compass

battery-powered clock mechanism*

\* Follow the clock's instructions for use and construction.

**1.** Glue a sheet of patterned paper to the bottom of the tissue box.

**2.** Cover all four sides of the box with a different sheet of patterned paper. Leave the top of the box (the side with the opening) uncovered.

**3.** Turn the top of the box towards you, then carefully make a hole in the middle of one side using a scissor blade (or awl), as shown.* Twist the scissors around to enlarge the hole slowly.

\* Ask an adult to do this for you.

**4.** Take the clock mechanism apart, noting down how to put the pieces back together again as you go. Insert it through the opening of the box and push the centre through the hole, as shown.

107

**5.** On another sheet of patterned paper, draw a circle with your compass slightly smaller than the width of the box. Cut out the circle, then use the blade to make a hole in the middle.

**6.** Glue the circle over the box, gently pushing the clock mechanism through the hole in the circular sheet of patterned paper.

**7.** Turn the box so the opening is now at the bottom, then stamp numbers around the inside of the circle. Start with 12 at the top, then 6 at the bottom, and add 3 and 9 on either side. Fill in the gaps with the other numbers.

**8.** Add and tighten the remaining clock parts on the mechanism, so that your clock starts to take shape.

depth of box

width of box

**9.** For the roof, cut a piece of patterned card into two pieces. These should be the same width as the front face of the box and slightly narrower than the depth of the box.

**10.** Create a tab on one roof piece by folding back the top edge by 1 cm. Cut a 15-cm piece of twine and form a loop as shown. Place the loop in the centre of the tab and add glue across the top.

**11.** Place the other strip over the top, press down firmly, then leave to dry. Trim the bottom edge of this strip to line up with the one underneath.

**12.** Cut another 15-cm piece of twine and thread three beads along the length. Tie a double knot below each bead to keep them in place. Feed the unknotted end of twine into the bottom of the box and glue it to the inside wall.

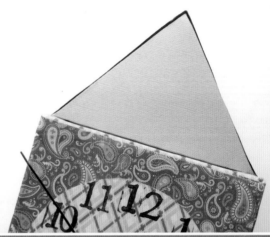

**13.** To attach the roof to the box, glue the edges on either side of the box (1 cm in from each edge).

**14.** To finish the roof, draw a triangle the same size and shape as the roof sides on a piece of card. Add a tab to each side of the triangle and cut out. Fold the tabs back and glue them inside the roof section.

**15.** Draw a bird shape and wing on different-patterned and -coloured card. Make the bird 1/3 the size of the width of the tissue box. Cut out the pieces.

**16.** Glue the bird wing to the body and then glue the body to the roof of the clock house. Now hang up your clock!

109

# SEWING PIN DREAMCATCHER

IT'S SEW DREAMY!

# MATERIALS

embroidery ring (inner hoop)

ball of wool

round-headed
sewing pins

scissors

**1.** Push the pins firmly into the hoop, 1.5 cm apart.*

*\* Ask an adult to help you.*

**2.** Wind the wool around the first pin, then loop the wool around a pin on the other side of the ring, tying a double knot to secure.

**3.** Keep weaving the wool back and forth, looping it around each pin (some more than once) until you are happy with the pattern. Tie a double knot around the last pin, to secure the wool in place. Cut off the ends with your scissors. Sweet dreams!

111

# SEAFARIN' PET PHOTO BOOTH

## MATERIALS

poster paints,
black marker pen,
paintbrush,
large cardboard box (slightly
bigger than your pet),
scissors,
dinner plate,
pencil,
all-purpose glue

1. Cut off the back of the cardboard box and put it aside for later. Unfold the top and bottom of the box, then flatten the remaining sides.

2. Place a large plate at the front of the box, 5 cm down from the top. This will act as a rough template for the size of hole you need for your pet's head to poke through. Draw around the plate.*

3. Now sketch the face of a bearded pirate, or sea captain, around the plate template. The face doesn't have to be the exact same shape as the template, but it should be no smaller. Leave out the facial features.

4. Draw the character's body, arms, legs and feet, then add paint and leave to dry.

5. Using the marker pen, go over the outlines to make your pirate or captain stand out.

6. Now carefully cut out your character's face, leaving the beard intact.

7. Draw a funny hat on the spare piece of cardboard, then paint it. Go over the outlines with the marker pen once dry. Cut it out, then glue the hat above the head on the box.

8. Stand up your seafarin' photo booth and guide your pet inside. Happy snapping!

\* The hole in the box needs to be large enough for your pet's head, to ensure it won't get stuck! Enlarge if necessary.

# MATERIALS

card circles x 2 (9 cm in diameter with 3 cm hole in the centre), green felt, green wool, red wool, scissors, white glue

## 1.
Cut a piece of red wool 500 cm long. Place the two rings together and wind the red wool through the centre hole until the wool no longer fits through.

## 2.
Insert the scissors between the card rings and trim the wool all the way around.

## 3.
Slip another piece of wool between the rings, and pull the ends tightly together. Tie it in a double knot.

## 4.
Now remove the card discs, and scrunch the wool to form a pom-pom.

## 5.
Trim the pom-pom into a cherry shape. Repeat steps 1 to 4 to make another two cherries.

## 6.
Cut out three pieces of dark green wool (each 15 cm long).

## 7.
Plait the wool by tying the strands together at one end, then cross the strand on the left over the one in the middle. Now cross the strand on the right over the one in the middle. Repeat the process until you reach the end of the wool, then tie a double knot.

## 8.
Make another two cherry stems, following step 7. Then cut out some leaf shapes from green felt.

## 9.
Glue the pom-poms and leaves onto the stems, as shown, then leave to dry. Finally, tie the cherries onto the handle of a bag!

SO CHERRY CUTE! →

# POM-POM CHERRY CHARMS

# A-MAZE-ING MARBLE GAME

AVOID
THE
TRAPS!

## MATERIALS

shoebox lid,
dark blue paper (large enough
to fit inside the shoebox lid),
construction paper
(light blue, yellow, white,
red and black),
coloured craft sticks,
pencil,
compass,
scissors,
ruler,
glue stick,
glue gun,
marble

↵

**1.**
Draw 48 squares (each 3 cm
x 3 cm) onto the pale blue
construction paper, then cut
them out.

**2.**
Glue the pale blue squares
onto the dark blue paper in a
chequerboard pattern.

**3.**
Repeat until you have covered
the entire sheet.

**4.**
Now use your compass to draw the
following circles on the other sheets of
construction paper:
five red and two black
(each 4.5 cm in diameter),
five white and two yellow
(each 4 cm in diameter),
five red (each 3.5 cm in diameter)
and one black (1.5 cm in diameter).

**5.**
Next, carefully cut out all of the circles from the construction paper.

**6.**
Glue the different circles together, matching the colours and sizes to the picture on the right. You should end up with seven circles in total.

**7.**
Use the compass to draw another circle in the middle of each red-and-white circle (2 cm in diameter). Then cut them out. These will be the traps!

**8.**
Place the chequerboard inside the shoebox lid (but don't stick it down just yet, as you'll need to cut out holes for the 'traps' in step 11). Glue the yellow-and-black circles on top, as shown. These are the start and finish points of your maze game.

**9.**
Now place the red-and-white circles in the same positions as pictured on the left, but don't glue them down.

**10.**
Use a pencil to trace around the inside of each hole onto the chequerboard, as shown. Then remove the red-and-white circles.

**11.**
Remove the chequerboard from the shoebox lid, then cut out inside the circles you have just drawn, to make holes. Now glue the chequerboard to the shoebox lid.

**12.**
Glue the red-and-white circles over the holes in the chequerboard, but make sure the holes are still visible.

**13.**
To create the walls of the maze, use the glue gun to run glue along one side of a craft stick.*

\* Ask an adult to use the glue gun in this step.

**14.**
Place the craft stick into position, as shown. Hold it in place for a few minutes until the glue is dry.

**15.**
Use the scissors to make shorter craft sticks, as shown, then repeat steps 13 to 14.

**16.**
Continue adding walls until your maze is complete. Write START on the yellow-and-black circle at the top, and FINISH on the one at the bottom. Place a marble on START, then tilt the game around as you guide your marble to the FINISH!

## MATERIALS
black and blonde hairgrips x 240,
jewellery wire, jewellery closure, jump ring,
jewellery pliers, wire clippers

### 1.
Cut three pieces of wire to the following lengths: 55 cm, 65 cm and 85 cm. Slip eight black hairgrips over the middle of the shortest piece of wire. Now add three blonde hairgrips to each side, as shown.

### 2.
Repeat step 1 until you have nine black hairgrip sections and ten blonde hairgrip sections on the same piece of wire.

### 3.
Do the same on the two remaining pieces of wire, but alternate the patterns however you like.

### 4.
Now line up all three wires, then insert the ends on the left through the jewellery closure. Fold the wires over, 3 cm down from the closure.

3 cm

### 5.
Use the pliers to wrap the ends around the wires, securing the closure in place. Trim away any excess with the clippers, as shown.

### 6.
Now insert the other end of the wires through the jump ring. Fold them over 3 cm down from the ring, then use the pliers to wrap the ends around the wires, securing the ring in place. Trim off any excess.

### 7.
Finally, secure the hairgrips in place by wrapping a small piece of wire around each side of the first line, as shown.

# GET-A-GRIP NECKLACE

GET GRIPPY
WITH IT!

# MATERIALS

coat hook rail, card, white craft foam, ankle socks x 4,
scissors, toy stuffing, all-purpose glue*,
black marker pen, compass, pencil

* Ask an adult to help use the all-purpose glue in steps 3 and 9!

**1.** Cut the ankle seam (or ribbed edging) off each
sock and put them aside for later.

**2.** Turn one sock inside out and draw a semicircle
just below the toe seam. Cut it out.

**3.** Run a trail of all-purpose glue around the edge
of the semicircle. Fold the rough edges back and
press into the glue.

7 cm

sock width

**4.** Draw a rounded rectangle onto the white
craft foam, 7 cm long and the same width as
the sock. Cut it out.

**5.** Turn the sock the right way out and place
the white craft foam in front of the semicircle.
Fill the sock with toy stuffing behind the craft
foam, and leave a gap at the end.

* Ask an adult to remove the hook and replace it on the rail for you!

**6.** Measure the hook width and add an extra 1 cm. Using the compass, draw and cut out a card circle matching this size. Remove the hook from the rail, then trace around the base in the centre of the circle.* Snip a slot at the bottom of the circle, then cut out the shape.

**7.** Use this circle as a template to create three more (ready for the other ninjas). Place your ninja character face-down and slide one circle inside it at a 45° angle. Make sure the slot is at the bottom.

**8.** Tuck the end of the sock inside the hole. Use your fingers to push the sock and toy stuffing down, to keep the hole open.

**9.** Now choose a sock seam from step 1 to create the headband. Roll the sock seam so that any rough edges are hidden inside, then glue it to the ninja's head, above its face.

**10.** Draw a ninja face on the white craft foam using your marker pen.

**11.** Repeat steps 2 to 5 for the other three socks. Then slot the card shapes made in step 7 inside the ninjas, and repeat steps 8 to 10. Slide your ninjas over the hooks, then hang up the rail, ready to use.*

* Ask an adult to do this for you!

# MATERIALS
empty juice carton, acrylic paints (white, blue and orange), paintbrushes, pencil, craft knife, black marker pen, white glue

## 1.
Make sure the juice carton is empty, then glue down the lid.* Add two coats of white acrylic paint, allowing to dry between each coat.

*\* Ask an adult to rinse the carton thoroughly with water and washing-up liquid.*

## 2.
Use a pencil to sketch the design of your shop onto the sides of the box.

## 3.
Paint over the pencil in blue and orange. Don't worry about being too neat at this stage.

## 4.
Now use your marker pen to carefully draw around the outlines and fill in the details.

## 5.
Use the craft knife to cut a small slot in the top of the carton to pop your money through.* Happy saving!

*\* Ask an adult to do this for you.*

STASH YOUR CASH!

COOL CARTON MONEY BOX

# STRING-MÂCHÉ GARLAND

IT'S A STRING THING!

# MATERIALS

coloured string, balloons x 8, white glue, water, bowl, large deep bowl, long wooden skewer, scissors, ruler (30 cm long)

## 1.

Cut out a length of string, 500 cm in total. Tie a slip knot at one end. Mix ¾ white glue with ¼ water in a bowl. Now place the string in the mixture, leaving the slip knot end out of the bowl.

## 2.

Inflate one of the balloons to 12 cm long and tie a knot at the end. Next loop the string's slip knot over the knot of the balloon.

## 3.

Carefully wrap the glue-covered string around the balloon. Feed the string through your fingers, to remove any excess glue as you go.

## 4.

Keep wrapping until all of the string is used. Tuck the end of the string under another piece of string, to secure it in place.

## 5.

Next thread the skewer carefully through the knot at the top of the balloon. Be careful not to puncture the balloon! Then hang it over a large bowl. Wait until the glue is clear and dry (this will take a few hours).

## 6.

Use the skewer to pop the balloon, then remove the balloon from the string ball. Repeat steps 1 to 6 until you have eight string balls.

## 7.

Cut a 200-cm piece of string and thread through the slip knot loop of one ball. Now slide the ball along the piece of string, leaving 30 cm at the end. Tie double knots on either side, to keep the ball in place. Continue to add more balls, placing them 20 cm apart from each other, until you have finished the garland.

# TAPE-OMIZED CABLES 'N' CASES

Give your gadgets a tape-over with these simple ideas, using versatile duct tape!*

RING! RING!

STRIPE-SATIONAL!

* Duct tape may leave a permanent mark on your belongings if removed.

Jazz up an old pair of earphones by winding a long, thin piece of duct tape around the cable, creating a fab 'n' funky spiral pattern.

Bring your charger up to date with a cool colour-block pattern. Just cut two contrasting coloured tapes into chunky square pieces, then wrap them around the cord, alternating the colours as you go!

For a dazzling, stripy tablet case, try alternating coloured tape with thick and thin strips, and opt for a diagonal pattern. To make your tablet really zing, leave a small gap between each strip! Don't forget to trim off the edges to finish.

Upcycle your phone case with a super-stylish chevron pattern! Place a rectangular piece of tape at the base of the phone, then overlap different-coloured triangular pieces all the way to the top. You've got it covered!

# IN-THE-FRAME LAMPSHADE

**LET IT GLOW!**

# MATERIALS
frames with plastic panes x 4, white glue, food colouring, small empty plastic bottles, scissors, all-purpose glue, lamp base, black card, paper

## 1.
Clean the bottles, then squeeze some glue into each one. Next add 15 ml of food colouring – one colour per bottle. Screw the lids on tightly and shake each bottle thoroughly to mix.

## 2.
Remove the plastic panes from the frames. Cover your work area with a plastic sheet or newspaper and then squeeze the coloured glue from each bottle onto the plastic panes.

## 3.
Place a sheet of paper on top and gently spread the coloured glue around. Remove the paper and leave the pane to dry. Repeat steps 2 and 3 for the other panes.

## 4.
On the back of a frame, dot some glue in each corner. Place a pane onto the glue and press down firmly so the pane sticks to the frame. Repeat for the other frames and panes.

## 5.
Cut the black card into four long strips, all the same length as the longer sides of the frame and around 3 cm wide.

3 cm

strip of black card

## 6.
Place two frames side by side, then glue a strip of black card over the two touching edges to join. Repeat for the other two frames, then join the two coupled frames together (side by side) with a third strip of black card.

final strip of black card

## 7.
Stand the frames up in a cube, with the card strips on the inside. Glue the final strip to the two unjoined edges. Now place over your lamp!

## MATERIALS
sticky back plastic, photo,
glitter stars and flakes, scissors,
clean jar with lid,* water

\* Ask an adult to clean the jar in a dishwasher
or with hot water and washing-up liquid.

**1.**
Cover both sides of the photo with
sticky back plastic, as shown.

**2.**
Trim the edges, but make
sure the photo is completely
covered in plastic.

MAKE THEM SPARKLE!

# GLITTER STORM PHOTOS

**3.**
Place the photo upside down inside the jar and at the back. Add the glitter stars and flakes.

**4.**
Fill the jar with water, and put the lid on tightly.

**5.**
Shake your jar and enjoy your fab photo glitter storm!

# ELE-BOX
# BOOKENDS

ELEPHANT-ASTIC!

137

Stop your books from falling off the shelf with these fab 'n' functional elephant bookends!

**MATERIALS**

newspaper, masking tape, sealed sandwich bags filled with dried rice, coloured paper, water, bowl, white glue, all-purpose glue,* pencil, paintbrush, scissors, wrapping paper, cereal boxes

* Ask an adult to help use the all-purpose glue in steps 9, 10 and 14!

**1.**
For one side of the elephant's body, draw a semicircle onto an opened-out cereal box. Sketch two smaller semicircles inside it for the legs and trunk. See measurements on the left. Then cut along the pencil lines.

**2.**
Use this as a template to trace the other side of the elephant onto another box. Then cut it out.

**3.**
Next cut out three squares from the cereal box card. Each square will need to be 5 cm in height and the same width as the legs and trunk. Tape in place on one side, at the bottom, as shown. Repeat for the other side of the elephant.

**4.**
Cut a strip of card 5 cm wide, making sure it's long enough to curve over the top of the elephant's body. Secure in place with lots of small pieces of tape, as shown.

**5.**
Cut a shorter strip of card, again 5 cm wide, and tape it to the inside of the legs, as shown.

**6.**
Take the sandwich bags (containing dried rice), and place them inside the elephant to give it weight. Continue to add bags of rice until the inside of the elephant is full. Now tape a strip of card (5 cm wide) between the front legs and trunk.

138

**7.**
Mix ¾ white glue with ¼ water in a bowl. Paste small sections of the mixture onto the elephant, sticking on strips of newspaper as you go. Brush another layer of glue over the top of the newspaper. Leave to dry.

**8.**
Use your elephant as a template to cut out two sheets of wrapping paper, but make them 2 cm wider all around.

**9.**
Use the glue mixture to stick the wrapping paper over the newspaper. Cut small flaps into the excess edges of wrapping paper, 2 cm apart, as shown. Then fold the flaps flat against the elephant and stick down with the all-purpose glue.

**10.**
Keep going until you've glued down all the flaps.

**11.**
Cut strips of wrapping paper, 5 cm wide, and use the glue mixture to stick the paper over the top of the elephant and inside its trunk and legs.

**12.**
Cut two semicircles from grey coloured paper for the ears. Make a fold 1 cm up from the bottom edge of each ear. Cut two circles for eyes.

**13.**
Cut a tail shape from blue coloured paper.

**14.**
Dab all-purpose glue onto the tail and along the folds of each ear, then stick them to the elephant. Repeat the steps to make another elephant bookend!

COOL IN CREPE!

# PAPER RA-RA SKIRT

Make a nifty no-sew skirt! Simply cut out, fold and glue your way to fashion fabulousness with this 1980s throw-back skirt made from crepe paper!

**MATERIALS**

crepe paper
x 3 (each
50 cm wide)

measuring
tape

self-adhesive
hook-
and-loop
fastener

scissors

pencil

glue gun*

ribbon
(4 cm wide)

**1.** Measure your waist, then cut a piece of ribbon to the same length as your waist measurement, plus an additional 20 cm.

**2.** Cut each piece of crepe paper to the same length as the ribbon.

**3.** Draw a line 14 cm from the bottom edge of one sheet of crepe paper.

**4.** Fold the crepe paper up to the marked line.

**5.** Place a little bit of glue 5 cm away from the bottom right-hand edge of the folded paper.

**6.** Now fold the paper lengthways, making a pleat all the way up to the top of the paper. Press firmly at the bottom of the pleat, so it sticks to the glue.

**7.** Repeat steps 5 and 6, gluing and folding pleats all the way along the paper, until you reach the left-hand edge.

**8.** Now draw a line 8 cm from the bottom edge of another sheet of crepe paper.

**9.** Fold the crepe paper up to the marked line.

**10.** Repeat steps 5 to 7 until this piece of crepe paper has also been pleated.

**11.** For the last piece of crepe paper, jump straight to steps 5 to 7, as it does not need to be folded at the bottom.

**12.** Now that all of the paper has been pleated, lay them on top of each other, as shown. Glue them together along the top edges.

hook closure   loop closure

**13.** Now glue all the way along the ribbon, then place it over the top edge of the skirt. Line up the right-hand side of the ribbon with the right-hand side of the paper. Some ribbon will be left over on the left-hand side, as shown.

**14.** Turn the skirt over, then fold in half. Separate the hook-and-loop fastener. Stick the hook closure on top of the ribbon on the right-hand side of the skirt. Then add the loop closure to the underside of the ribbon (sticking out in the picture above).

**15.** Wrap the skirt around your waist, then join the hook-and-loop fastener together.

**16.** Wear leggings or shorts beneath your fab ra-ra skirt!

## MATERIALS

square cream cushion (zip opening), fabric pens (black, white and orange),* pencil, black marker pen, scissors, needle, cream thread, cream felt, white card (similar size to cushion), sewing pins

*\* Follow the fabric pen instructions.*

### 1.
Use a pencil to copy this fox picture (right) onto the white card. Then draw over the lines with a marker pen.

### 2.
Remove the padding from the cushion cover and slide the white card inside. You should be able to see your fox drawing through the cushion cover. Trace over the design using the fabric pens. Use the white pen first, then the orange, and finish with the black.

### 3.
Fold the cream felt in half and draw a triangular ear shape, as shown.

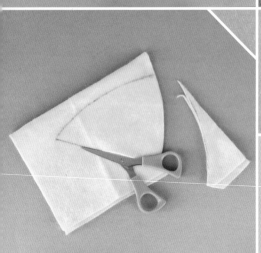

### 4.
Keeping the felt folded, cut out the ear shape. You will now have two symmetrical fox ears.

### 5.
Use the fabric pens to create the ear design (right). Wait for the fabric pens to dry before moving onto the next step.

### 6.
Roughly work out where you want the ears to be, then pin them in place on the back of the cushion cover. Sew on the ears using two rows of simple running stitches.

### 7.
Remove the card template and slide the padding back inside the cushion cover. So cute!

# FACE-THE-FOX CUSHION

HELP!

# RAIN CLOUD MOBILE

DRIP!
DROP!

## MATERIALS

scissors,
masking tape,
wire coat hanger,
invisible thread,
pencil,
black marker pen,
glue stick,
raindrop hole punch
(optional),
white card (A3 size),
blue paint swatches

**1.** Cut the swatches into strips, then use the hole punch (or scissors) to create around 100 raindrops.

**2.** Place the wire coat hanger over the white card. Sketch a cloud shape around the hanger, making it a little bigger than the hanger itself. Draw a face onto the cloud, using the marker pen, then cut out the cloud shape.

**3.** Cut seven pieces of invisible thread (70 cm each). Lay them on a work surface and stick masking tape at either end of the pieces to hold in place.

**4.** Add glue to the back of a raindrop shape. Place the raindrop under the thread, then stick another raindrop over the top, sandwiching the thread between the two raindrops.

**5.** Continue to add more raindrops to each piece of invisible thread, placing them evenly apart. Use masking tape to fix each line of raindrops to the back of the cloud, as shown.

**6.** Stick the wire coat hanger to the cloud using long strips of masking tape. Now you're ready to hang up your super-cool rain cloud mobile.

147

# MATERIALS

shrink plastic*,
black marker pen,
ruler,
scissors,
keyring,
baking tray,
greaseproof paper,
heavy book

* Follow the shrink plastic instructions.

**1.** Using your ruler and marker pen, draw a geometric shape on the shrink plastic.

**2.** Create a geometric pattern inside the outline, still using your ruler.

**3.** Colour areas of the pattern with your pen.

**4.** Cut out the shape, leaving a ½-cm gap around the edges, as shown. Cut a hole big enough to fit over your keyring once shrunk.

**5.** Place your design on a piece of greaseproof paper on a baking tray. Read the instructions for the shrink plastic, and put it in the oven.*

* Ask an adult to do this for you.

**6.** When your design has shrunk, take the tray out of the oven* and press a heavy book over the design. When cool, add a keyring through the hole.

* Ask an adult to do this for you.

148

**IT'S GEO-NIUS!**

# TASTIC RING

# MASTERPIECE

## MATERIALS

40 to 50 wax crayons
foam board (A3 size)
black construction paper
pencil
scissors
glue stick
glue gun*
hairdryer*

**1.** Draw a person holding an umbrella on black paper and cut out the shape. Now glue into place on the bottom left-hand corner of the foam board, 5 cm away from the side.

**2.** Stick the crayons across the top of the foam board using the glue gun, as shown.*

\* Ask an adult to do this step for you.

**3.** Put something behind the foam board so it stands up at a slight angle. Then turn on your hairdryer and point it at the first few crayons until they melt. Now point your hairdryer at the next few, and so on, until all the crayons have melted.**

\* Caution: glue guns are hot, so ask an adult to help!
\*\* Do not touch the crayons or the end of the hairdryer until cooled.

IT'S RAINING CRAYONS!

# TOP-DOG
# DRAUGHT EXCLUDER

## MATERIALS
long-sleeved stripy top, red felt, toy stuffing, needle, buttons x 2, pencil, pins, scissors, red and blue embroidery thread

**1.** Turn the top inside out and position it to match the above picture. Draw the shape of a dog's head on the body of the top, joining it to the arm (as shown). Add some pins just inside the pencil line through both sides of the top.

WOOF!

WOOF!

**2.** Carefully cut out the dog's head, following the pencil line as shown.

**3.** Line up the other sleeve alongside the one that has just been cut out. Cut off the second sleeve, just beneath the dog's head on the first sleeve. Use the stripes to guide you. Now cut off both cuffs where the sleeves start to narrow.

**4.** Turn the second sleeve inside out and push it inside the arm of the first sleeve (with the dog's head). Line up the sleeve ends.

**5.** Pin the sleeves together through the first two layers of fabric around the entire sleeve circumference. Sew a stretch stitch just inside the pinned lines (but don't sew the sleeves closed). Remove the pins.

**6.** Now stretch stitch just inside the pins around the head shape. Remove the pins.

**7.** Turn your dog the right way out (the second sleeve added in step 4 will also be pulled out). Fill the dog with toy stuffing.

**8.** Leave 15 cm from the end unstuffed for the tail. Squeeze the fabric together, as shown.

**9.** Tie a knot as close as possible to the stuffing.

154

**10.** Fold the piece of felt in half and draw three rectangles with rounded ends along the folded edge.

**11.** Carefully cut out each rectangle.

**12.** Unfold two pieces of felt, and place at both ends of the body for legs, as shown. Pin the legs in place, then sew a running stitch along the centre of each felt piece to attach them.

**13.** Cut the remaining piece of felt in half (along the fold) to make a pair of ears.

**14.** Pin an ear to each side of the dog's head. Sew each ear on with a running stitch at the top. Remove the pins.

**15.** Now sew the button eyes on each side of the head. What a paw-fect pooch!

* Ask an adult to help use the varnish in step 5!

## MATERIALS
pebbles x 10, paintbrush, black marker pen, acrylic paints, correction fluid pen, clear varnish,* black paper, chalk

**1.** Paint five blue pebbles, then five orange pebbles, using acrylic paint. Leave to dry.

**2.** To create a monster face, blob two eyes on a blue pebble with correction fluid. Leave to dry.

**3.** Add the pupils and mouth with the marker pen. Then paint some gappy teeth using the correction fuid.

**4.** Create different funny monster faces on the remaining nine pebbles, as shown.

**5.** Varnish the pebbles for protection, then draw a grid of 3 x 3 squares on black paper with chalk. Play with a friend, choosing to be either blue or orange. Take turns to place your pebbles on the grid. The first to get three same-coloured pebbles in a row wins!

# NOUGHTS 'N' MONSTERS

MAKE A MONSTER MOVE WITH THESE REBEL PEBBLES!

# PEN-CHANTING PATTERNS

Customize your things with some simple pen designs.
Stamp your style on caps, lunch boxes or whatever you like!

Upcycle a plain glass into a work of art using a glass pen. Why not add a stray square in a spotty pattern and see if your friends can find it!?

Fabric pens are a fab way to customize clothes. Experiment with different patterns, and maybe add a twist. Can you spot the rebellious arrow in this design?

Create a simple cross-hatch patterned lunch box with a permanent marker pen.

Ballpoint pens are a brilliant doodle tool for stationery. Try different doodly designs on folders, notepads and diaries.

Give a dark frame a super-snazzy pattern using white correction fluid!

Storage boxes don't have to be boring! Bring yours to life with a chalk marker and some triangular patterns.

Metallic marker pens are great for giving a shimmery finish, like on this patterned pencil case.

# EYE SPOT A PEACOCK

**FANCY TAIL!**

## MATERIALS
scissors,
black pen,
all-purpose glue,
patterned fabric scraps,
stretched plain canvas,
white card (half the
size of the canvas),
craft foam (similar size to
the white card)

↵

\* Ask an adult to help use the all-purpose
glue in steps 3 and 4!

**1.**
Draw a peacock body and leaf
shape for feathers onto a sheet of
card and cut out as templates for
this craft. Use the template to draw
the peacock body and 14 leaf
feathers onto a sheet of foam. Then
cut them out.

**2.**
Draw a larger and smaller oval
onto the sheet of card and cut
out as a template for the eye
feathers on the peacock. Now use
these templates to create 13 large
eye feathers and 26 small eye
feathers from the different types of
patterned fabric.

**3.**
Next glue the peacock body to
the middle of the canvas. Add
some large and small eye feathers
around it.

**4.**
Glue some of the small eye
feathers in the middle of the larger
ones. Now add the leaf feathers
around the outside to finish.
What a pretty peacock!

161

## MATERIALS

flat-packed cardboard boxes x 7 (30 cm x 23 cm x 26 cm), ruler, pencil, scissors, twine, black marker pen

**1.** Label the boxes 1 to 7 in pencil. Take box 1 and cut three ½ cm wide slots (from top to middle), as shown.

**2.** Draw two doorways, one on each side of the box (15 cm x 20 cm), then carefully cut them out. Cut off the two top flaps.

**3.** Turn over the box. Draw battlements (4 cm wide) on the two top flaps, then cut them out.

**4.** Use some of the waste card to make a window template (10 cm x 5 cm) with a rounded top, then cut it out. Use your template to draw three windows on the two sides of the box facing upwards, then carefully cut them out.

**5.** Add detail on the two sides of the box, such as ivy and bricks, using your pen.

holes

20 cm

15 cm

½ cm    ½ cm    ½ cm

②

**6.** Take box 2 and cut three ½ cm wide slots (from bottom to middle), as shown. Draw a drawbridge on the left side of the box (15 cm x 20 cm), then cut out the top and sides, and fold down the bottom. Make four holes on the card, as shown.

4 cm

15 cm

20 cm

②

**7.** Thread two pieces of twine (each 30 cm long) through the holes to make the drawbridge chains. Tie knots at either end. Create a doorway on the right side of the box and battlements on the left top flap. Add detail using your pen.

15 cm    15 cm

20 cm    20 cm

½ cm    ②

**8.** Turn over the box and cut a ½ cm wide slot (from bottom to middle), as shown. Create two doorways, one on each side of the box.

4 cm

½ cm    ½ cm

15 cm

20 cm

③

**9.** Take box 3 and cut two ½ cm wide slots (from top to middle), as shown. Create a doorway on the left side of the box, then cut off the left top flap. Create battlements on the right top flap and two windows on the right side of the box. Add detail using your pen.

4 cm    ½ cm

15 cm

20 cm

③

**10.** Turn over the box and cut a ½ cm wide slot (from top to middle), as shown. Create battlements on the left top flap and a window on the left side of the box. Create a doorway on the right side of the box, then cut off the right top flap. Add detail.

4 cm

15 cm

20 cm

½ cm    ½ cm    ④

**11.** Take box 4 and cut two ½ cm wide slots (from bottom to middle), as shown. Create a doorway on the left side of the box, then cut off the left top flap. Create battlements on the right top flap and two windows on the right side of the box. Add detail.

**12.** Turn over the box and cut a ½ cm wide slot (from bottom to middle), as shown. Create battlements on the left top flap and a window on the left side of the box. Create a doorway on the right side of the box, then cut off the right top flap. Add detail.

**13.** Take box 5 and cut three ½ cm wide slots (from top to middle), as shown. Create battlements on the left top flap and a window on the left side of the box. Create a doorway on the right side of the box. Add detail.

**14.** Turn over the box and cut a ½ cm wide slot (from top to middle), as shown. Create two doorways, one on each side of the box.

**15.** Take box 6 and cut three ½ cm wide slots (from bottom to middle), as shown. Create two doorways, one on each side of the box, then cut off the two top flaps.

**16.** Turn over the box. Create battlements on the two top flaps and three windows on the two sides of the box. Add detail.

**17.** Take box 7 and cut a ½ cm wide slot (from bottom to fold line) halfway across the width of the right bottom flap, as shown. Create a doorway on the left side of the box, battlements on the two top flaps and two windows on the right side of the box. Add detail.

**18.** Turn over the box and cut a ½ cm wide slot (from bottom to fold line) halfway across the width of the right bottom flap, as shown. Create battlements on the two top flaps and three windows on the two sides of the box. Add detail.

**19.** Stand boxes 1 to 6 in the order shown. Make sure the decorated sides face out. Lift box 2 above the others and slide it into the slots of boxes 1, 3 and 5. Carefully push box 2 down so the slots interlock and it becomes level with the other boxes.

**20.** Lift box 4 above the others and slide it into the slots of boxes 1 and 5. Push box 4 down so the slots interlock. Now slide box 6 into the slots of boxes 3 and 5. Push box 6 down so the slots interlock.

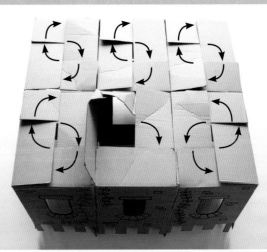

**21.** Turn the castle upside down, carefully resting the battlements on the floor. Interlock the flaps on the base of each box, as shown.

**22.** Turn the castle the right way round, and fold the top flaps of boxes 2 and 5 inwards to form another floor.

**23.** Lift box 7 above the 'floor' and slide the longer bottom flaps into boxes 1 and 4 (on one side), and 3 and 6 (on the other). Lay the smaller bottom flaps on the 'floor'!

167

pair of gloves, needle, thread, scissors,
toy stuffing, small coloured buttons x 2,
big white buttons x 2, black marker pen

**1.**

Turn the gloves inside out, then draw
a curved line at the top of each
glove to make a rough body shape,
as shown.

**2.**

Carefully cut along the curved lines.

**3.**

Draw another curved line 2 cm
up from the fingers of each glove.
Remove the top 'layer' of each
glove by cutting the side seams
down and along each line. Both
gloves should now have one long
layer and one short layer.

**4.**

Using a running stitch, sew the
gloves together (with the shorter
layers on the inside). Sew around
the edges, starting and ending
just above the fingers.

**5.**

Open out the gloves, as shown.
Sew together the section between
the fingers with a running stitch.
Leave a 2-cm gap at one end for
the stuffing.

**6.**

Turn the gloves inside out so the
stitching is hidden. Fill your octopus
with stuffing, then close up the gap
from step 5 using a running stitch.

**7.**

To finish, sew on some button eyes.
Stitch the big white buttons on
first, then add the small coloured
buttons on top.

I GLOVE YOU!

GLOVE
OCTO

169

## MATERIALS

strips of coloured paper,
frame, card (to fit inside frame),
quilling tool, pencil, black marker pen,
white glue, plate

### 1.

First turn the strips of paper into
spirals. Slot the end of one piece
of paper into the quilling tool, then
twirl it around.

### 2.

When the entire strip of paper has
been curled into a tight roll, carefully
remove it from the quilling tool.

### 3.

Dab some glue on the end of
the spiral to stick it together, then
leave to dry. Continue making
quilled spirals until you have
about 60 or 70 altogether.

### 4.

Draw a circle for the hot-air balloon
and a small basket below onto
some card. Attach the basket to
the balloon and add a character
in the basket!

### 5.

Use the pen to draw over everything
apart from the balloon. Sketch some
clouds using the pen, to give your
picture extra detail.

### 6.

Pour the glue onto a plate, then
dip the edge of a spiral into the
glue. Now stick the spiral onto the
balloon shape, as shown.

### 7.

Continue adding more spirals until
the balloon is completely covered.
Leave to dry, then frame your hot-air
balloon picture and hang it up!*

\* Ask an adult to help.

# COSY CROCHET TABLET CASE

# MATERIALS

sewing machine, fabric x 2, wadding, wool, crochet hook, scissors, needle, thread, pins, button

## 1.

To make a slip knot, create a loop in the wool, as shown. Insert the hook through the loop and hook under the tail. Pull the tail to tighten the wool around the hook, creating a loop on the hook.

## 2.

To make a chain stitch, bring the wool over the hook (from back to front) and hook it. Draw the hooked wool through the loop on the hook.

## 3.

Repeat step 2 five more times, to make 6 chain stitches in total.

## 4.

To make a slip stitch (in order to create a ring), insert the hook through the first chain stitch, then bring the wool over the hook (from back to front) and hook it. Draw the hooked wool through both the stitch and the loop on the hook.

## 5.

Repeat step 2 three times to make 3 chain stitches in total.

## 6.

To make a treble crochet stitch, bring the wool over the hook (from back to front), then insert the hook through the centre of the ring. Bring the wool over the hook (from back to front) and hook it.

## 7.

Pull the hook back through the centre of the ring. You should now have three loops on the hook.

## 8.

Now bring the wool over the hook (from back to front) and hook it. Draw the hooked wool through two loops on the hook. You should now have two loops on the hook.

## 9.

Now bring the wool over the hook (from back to front) and hook it. Draw the hooked wool through both loops on the hook. You've finished your treble crochet stitch!

173

**10.**
Repeat steps 6 to 9 ten times to make 11 treble crochet stitches in total.

**11.**
To finish this row, make a slip stitch through the top of the 3 chain stitches (see step 4).

b

c

a

**12.**
Now you're ready to start the second row! First, repeat step 2 three times to make 3 chain stitches in total.

**13.**
Repeat steps 6 to 9 twice to make 2 treble crochet stitches in the first gap in the row below. Then repeat step 2 to make 1 chain stitch.

b

a

**14.**
Repeat step 13 to make 11 more sets of 2 treble crochet stitches followed by 1 chain stitch.

**15.**
To finish this row, make a slip stitch through the top of the 3 chain stitches (see step 4).

b

a

**16.**
Now you're ready to start the third row! First, repeat step 2 three times to make 3 chain stitches in total.

**17.**
Repeat steps 6 to 9 twice to make 2 treble crochet stitches in the first gap (between each pair of treble crochet stitches) in the row below. Then repeat step 2 twice to make 2 chain stitches.

**18.**
Repeat step 17 to make 11 more sets of 2 treble crochet stitches followed by 2 chain stitches.

**19.**
To finish this row, make a slip stitch through the top of the 3 chain stitches (see step 4).

**20.**
Now you're ready to start the fourth and final row! Follow steps 16 to 19.

**21.**
To cast off, pull the loop on the hook (making it bigger). Remove the hook. Cut off the wool, then feed the end (or tail) through the loop, and pull tight. Use a needle to guide the two tails of wool through your work a few times.

**22.**
For the case, fold a piece of fabric in half (at the bottom), then lay the tablet on top. Cut the fabric, making it 2 cm larger all around than the case.

**23.**
Turn the fabric inside out (still folded). Pin the two long sides together and sew straight stitches down each one (½ cm from the edge).

**24.**
Follow steps 22 and 23 with the other fabric. Then cut out two pieces of wadding the same size as your tablet.

**25.**
Turn the two fabric pieces the right way round, then slide a piece of wadding inside each one.

**26.**
Now pin the two fabric pieces together, making sure the unsewn ends line up. Sew the unsewn end and the two longer sides of the case (½ cm from the edge), leaving the other shorter end unsewn.

**27.**
Turn the case the right way out, so the seams are on the inside. Check your tablet fits snugly inside.

**28.**
At the opening of the case, place half of your crochet circle over the top, as shown. Use a needle and thread to sew a simple running stitch from the crochet circle to the first fabric layer of your case.

**29.**
Stitch a button on the other side, then pop it through the crochet lid to close.

## MATERIALS

circular acrylic mirror, plastic spoons, all-purpose glue*

* Ask an adult to help use the all-purpose glue in each step!

**1.** Add a few drops of glue to the back of a spoon, then stick it onto the edge of the mirror. Keep adding more spoons, spacing them 1 cm apart from each other.

**2.** Continue sticking the spoons all around the mirror, alternating the colours as you go!

**3.** Now add a second layer of spoons, gluing them in-between the gaps from the first row. Continue until the outer edge of the mirror is hidden by spoons. When you've finished, hang it up!*

* Ask an adult to help

# SUPER SPOON MIRROR

**MIRROR, MIRROR ON THE WALL, WE'RE THE FAIREST SPOONS OF ALL!**

# CRANE ORIG-ARMY

FOLD A FLOCK OF PRETTY BIRDS!

# MATERIALS
patterned paper
(minimum 15 cm x 15 cm)

**1.**
a. Fold the paper diagonally in half
from top right to bottom left corner.
b. Now fold in half again,
from top left to bottom right.

**2.**
Fold the bottom right-hand corner
of the top flap of the triangle
across to the left.

**3.**
a. Open up and spread the top flap
out from the inside.
b. Fold it flat to make a square.

**4.**
Flip the paper over from right to left.
Fold the bottom left-hand corner
across to the right.
a. Open up and spread the new flap
out from the inside.
b. Fold it flat to make a square.

**5.**
a. Rotate the square 45° clockwise,
so the square looks like a diamond.
Then fold the right and left sides
into the centre.
b. Press the creases flat.

**6.**
a. Fold the top corner down to the
dotted line.
b. Now unfold the folds made in
steps 5 and 6a.

**7.**
a. Open the pocket by pulling the
top layer of paper from the bottom
of the diamond (point 1) up.
b. Points 2 and 3 should fold into
the centre. Press flat to make
an elongated diamond.

**8.**
Flip the paper over from right to left and repeat steps 5 to 7 on this side. However there is no need to rotate the square 45°.

a

b

**9.**
a. Fold the right and left sides into the centre.
b. Press the creases flat.

**10.**
Flip the paper over from right to left and repeat step 9 on this side.

**11.**
a. Fold the right point up to the dashed line. Then unfold.
b. Now separate the two layers of the right point. Guide the point up inside the two layers of paper.
c. Press the point flat at the crease. The right point should now be sandwiched between two layers of the body.

right point

a

b

body

right point

c

**12.**
Repeat step 11 for the left point.

**13.**
Fold the tip of the right point down, so that you form the beak.

**14.**
a. To make the wings, fold the top layer of the centre point down to reveal the body, and fold.
b. Now flip it over and repeat on the other side.

a

b

**15.**
To finish, spread the wings out by pulling them slightly away from each other. Make as many cranes as you like, then chain them together on a string!

181

STAMP
IT
OUT!

# FABU-MASH
# PINEAPPLE PRINT

## MATERIALS

paper plates,
fabric paints*,
old T-shirt,
potato masher,
fork

* Follow the fabric paint instructions.

**1.** Squeeze some fabric paint onto a paper plate. Place the potato masher in the paint, then spread it around to get an even coverage.

**2.** Now line up the masher with the bottom of the T-shirt and press down firmly.

**3.** Apply more paint to the masher before making a new stamp on the T-shirt. Then try adding different colours to your design. With each new colour, first rinse out the masher with water.

**4.** Take your fork and press the prongs into the fabric paint, making sure to cover the fork evenly.

**5.** Press the fork head to the top of each pineapple three times (to create a row). This makes the leaf detail.

**6.** Keep stamping until you're happy with your T-shirt design. Tee-rrific!

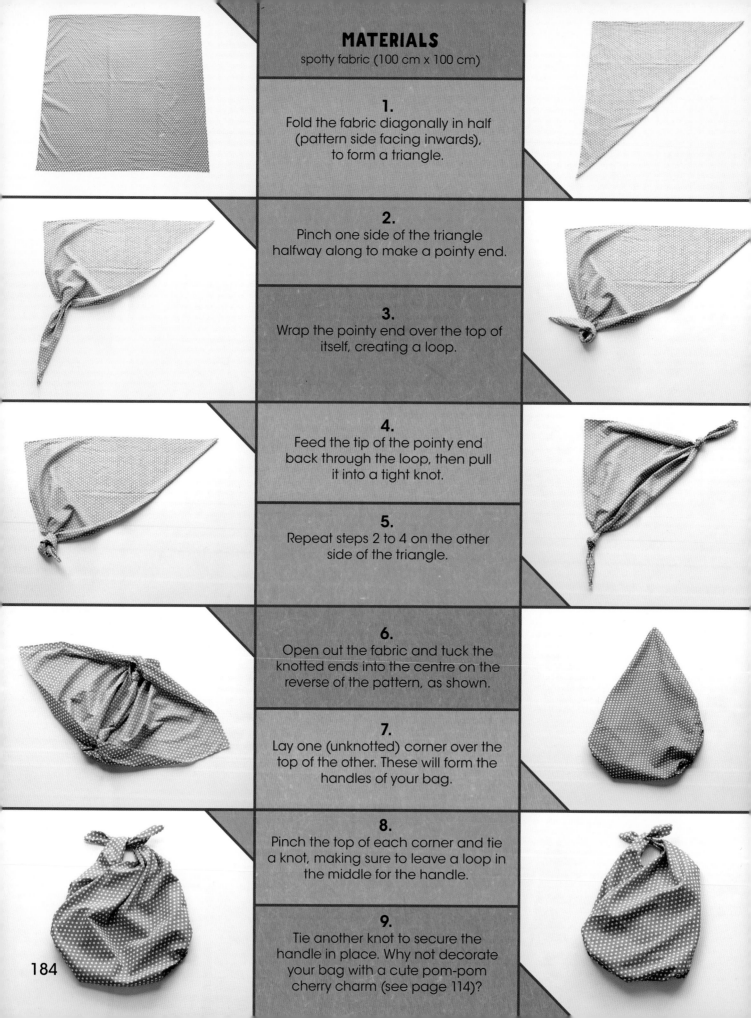

# MATERIALS
spotty fabric (100 cm x 100 cm)

## 1.
Fold the fabric diagonally in half (pattern side facing inwards), to form a triangle.

## 2.
Pinch one side of the triangle halfway along to make a pointy end.

## 3.
Wrap the pointy end over the top of itself, creating a loop.

## 4.
Feed the tip of the pointy end back through the loop, then pull it into a tight knot.

## 5.
Repeat steps 2 to 4 on the other side of the triangle.

## 6.
Open out the fabric and tuck the knotted ends into the centre on the reverse of the pattern, as shown.

## 7.
Lay one (unknotted) corner over the top of the other. These will form the handles of your bag.

## 8.
Pinch the top of each corner and tie a knot, making sure to leave a loop in the middle for the handle.

## 9.
Tie another knot to secure the handle in place. Why not decorate your bag with a cute pom-pom cherry charm (see page 114)?

WHAT'S KNOT
TO LIKE?

# SPOTTY
# KNOTTY
# BAG

Once upon a time, Little Red Riding Hood set off through the woods to visit her poorly grandmother. Along the way, she met a BIG BAD WOLF and... well, you know the rest! Try making these simple spoon puppets, then put on your very own fairy-tale puppet show.

## MATERIALS →

acrylic paints

paintbrush

wooden spoons

pencil

**1.** Draw Little Red Riding Hood's face and hood on a spoon, as shown. Sketch some lines for her cape.

**2.** Now paint the red hood and cape, then leave to dry.

**3.** Paint Little Red Riding Hood's black hair, features and bow. Then turn more spoons into the grandmother, hunter and Big Bad Wolf!

WHAT BIG **HEADS** YOU HAVE!

# FAIRY-TALE SPOON PUPPETS

# MATERIALS
unfolded cardboard box,
several different-coloured rolls of duct tape,
scissors, black paper, glue stick

## 1.
Lay the box on its side. Tape the two side flaps to the walls inside. This is so you can easily move your puppets around the theatre when it's finished.

## 2.
Fold the bottom flap upwards and tape it in place, as shown. Fold the top flap upwards, but leave untaped.

## 3.
Using the duct tape, decorate the front of the box in colourful stripes.

## 4.
Carry on adding the striped pattern around the outside and the inside of the box. This will create colourful edges at the front of the box.

## 5.
Finally, glue black paper to the insides of the box, as well as the top flap. This will give your theatre a professional finish. Draw a picture of some scenery for the backdrop, and it's showtime!

HE'S BEHIND
**YOU!**

MAKE 'EM
MELT!

## MATERIALS

baking foil,
oven tray,
cake tin ring,
star-shaped cookie cutters x 3,
round cookie cutters x 3,
small, fusible plastic beads*,
scissors,
thread

↵

* Beads must be suitable for craft making and for use with an iron or oven!

**1.**
Preheat the oven to 200°C.* Now line a baking tray with foil and place the star-shaped cookie cutters on top. Fill the cutters with beads, as shown.
* Ask an adult to do this for you.

**2.**
Put the tray in the oven for 10 minutes, and then remove.*
* Ask an adult to do this for you.

**3.**
Once cooled, remove the cutters from the star-shaped beads. Place the large cake tin ring inside the baking tray and around the stars. Add more coloured beads inside the ring, as shown, and repeat step 2.

**4.**
To make the smaller circles, follow steps 1 to 2, but use the round cookie cutters.

**5.**
Feed a piece of thread through the top of each bead circle. Now tie the bead shapes together (using a double knot), as shown. Hang your pretty suncatcher outside or in a window!

191

# COMIC STRIP TABLETOP

## MATERIALS
old comics, books or magazines
old, small table*
scissors
white glue
water
bowl
paintbrush

* Check with an adult first before using!

1. Mix ¾ white glue with ¼ water in a bowl.

2. Cut out pictures from the comics, books or magazines.

3. Paint a thin layer of the glue mixture onto a small area of the table, then stick on some of the cut-outs.

4. Repeat step 3 until the entire table is covered with cut-outs. Leave to dry.

5. To finish, brush another layer of glue mixture over the table to seal your design. Once dry, it's ready to use!

**MATERIALS**
strips of patterned paper,
old book,
butterfly hole punch
(optional),
sticky tack,
glue stick,
scissors (optional)

e

d      c

b      a

unfolded butterfly

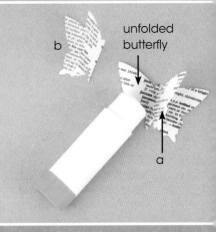

unfolded butterfly

b

a

**1.** Use the butterfly hole punch (or scissors) to create lots of butterfly shapes from the patterned paper and torn-out pages from the old book.

**2.** Take six butterflies. Fold five of them in half, as shown, a to e. Make sure the patterned (or printed) paper is on the inside.

**3.** Add glue to the wings of the unfolded butterfly. Press folded butterfly a onto the right side of the unfolded butterfly, matching the wing shapes together. Then press folded butterfly b onto the left side of the unfolded butterfly.

d

b

c

a

e

d

c

**4.** Add glue to the outer wings of butterflies a and b. Press butterfly c on top of a (on the right side), and butterfly d on top of b (on the left side).

**5.** Unfold butterfly e. Stick it on top of the outer wings of butterflies c and d, pattern side facing out.

**6.** Carefully fan out each wing to give your butterfly a 3D look. Add some sticky tack to the back of the butterfly and attac it to a wall. Repeat steps 2 to 6 until you have lots of pretty fluttering butterflies.

# FLUTTERING BUTTERFLIES

DON'T WORRY, BE FLAPPY!

# PIN CUSHION CACTUS

OUCH!

IT'S PRICKLY!

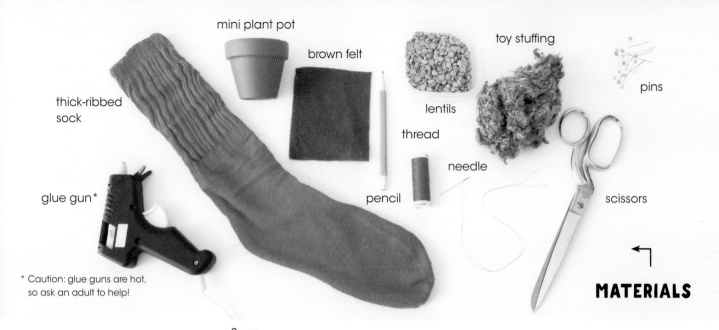

thick-ribbed
sock

glue gun*

* Caution: glue guns are hot,
so ask an adult to help!

mini plant pot

brown felt

lentils

thread

pencil

needle

toy stuffing

pins

scissors

**MATERIALS**

2 cm
(non-ribbed pattern)

**1.** Cut off the foot of the sock, leaving 2 cm of non-ribbed pattern at the end.

**2.** Fold the sock in half lengthways. Sew the two sides together with a running stitch, leaving the ends unstitched.

**3.** Now sew the top of the sock closed. First stitch together the inner layer, as shown, gathering all the stitches into a point.

**4.** Repeat step 3 for the outer layer of the sock.

197

**5.** Flip the sock inside out (push a pencil inside to help, if needed).

**6.** Fill the sock evenly with stuffing, then set aside.

**7.** To create the 'soil', place the pot upside down on the brown felt and trace around it.

**8.** Use your scissors to cut out the circle.

**9.** Fold the circle in half and make a 1.5-cm snip in the middle. Fold in half the other way and repeat.

**10.** The felt should now have two slots forming a cross, as shown.

**11.** Insert the bottom (unstitched) section of the sock through the felt.

**12.** Now add a good amount of glue in the bottom of the pot.*

*\* Ask an adult to do this for you.*

**13.** Firmly press the unstitched end of the sock into the glue.

**14.** Fill the pot with dried lentils to prevent the cactus from tipping over.

**15.** Glue all around the inner edge of the pot,* then stick the edges of brown felt over the glue.

*\* Ask an adult to do this for you.*

**16.** Now push your pins into the sock to complete your pin cushion cactus. Spiky!

# MATERIALS

plain file folder,
stamps,
pencil,
scissors,
glue stick,
white vinyl sticky paper

**1.**
Line up your folder with the bottom right corner of the vinyl paper.

**2.**
Draw around the folder onto the back of the paper.

**3.**
Sketch the outline of an elephant (or whatever animal you like) in the centre of the folder shape.

**4.**
Carefully cut out the folder and elephant shapes.

**5.**
Place the vinyl paper over the folder, lining up the edges. Trace around the elephant onto the folder, then remove the paper. Stick the stamps onto the folder, covering the elephant.

**6.**
Place the vinyl paper back over the folder, but this time slowly peel away the sticky backing. Smooth the paper down so it sticks to the folder, revealing your stamp-tastic design!

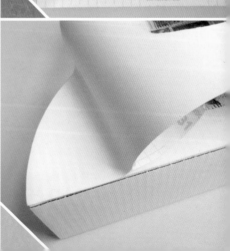

# STAMP-IMAL FOLDER

**NELLY THE ELE-STAMP!**

**STAMP!** **STOMP!** **STAMP!**

# PAPER BEAD
# BRACELET

WEAVE
AND WEAR!

# MATERIALS

coloured paper (A4 size),
scissors, ruler, needle, twine

## 1.

Cut each sheet of paper into
½-cm wide strips. Fold one strip in half
widthways. Use the crease to help
you form a point at the centre, as
shown. Do the same on another strip.

## 2.

Now weave the two pieces together, as
shown, pulling them tightly so the two
folded points hook together.

## 3.

Begin weaving the four strips
together as follows:
a. Pull the strip on the far left
over the strip to the right of it.
b. Pull the strip on the far right under
the strip to the left of it, then over the
next strip to the left. Pull taut so the
paper curves. Repeat this step six
more times, until you have a ball.

## 4.

To secure, pull the strip on the far
left under a strip on the paper ball
(the one closest to it).

## 5.

Pull this strip out the other side of
the one on the ball, as shown.
Trim the strip to align it with the
shape of the ball.

## 6.

Repeat steps 4 and 5 for the other
three strips to form a ball; first with the
far right strip, then the remaining left
strip, then the remaining right strip.

## 7.

Then repeat steps 1 to 5 until you have
enough beads to go around your
wrist. Thread the twine through the
needle, and slide on the beads. Finish
by tying your paper bracelet to your
wrist with a double knot!

far left strip

# FLOOR SNAKES AND LADDERS

FINISH

START

SNAKE, RATTLE AND ROLL!

## MATERIALS

masking tape,
brown, green, yellow and red rolls of washi tape,
scissors,
tape measure,
ruler

* Ask an adult for permission before doing this craft.

**1.** To make a giant-sized version of this popular board game, first create a square (each side 182 cm) on the floor with masking tape.

**2.** Stick another five strips of masking tape (each 182 cm long) vertically inside the square, as shown. Leave a gap of 30 cm between each strip.

**3.** Repeat step 2, but this time place the strips horizontally, to form a grid of 36 squares in total. Now you're ready to create the numbers for the board game.

4. Before you make the numbers, note the order, shown on pages 204–205.

5. Now create the numbers using masking tape. Try to keep them roughly the same size for each digit (15 cm high and 10 cm wide). See the pictures above for help.

6. Place the numbers, one at a time, in the middle of each square as you go. For numbers made up of two digits, leave a gap of 2 cm between each digit.

7. To make a ladder, first cut two strips of brown washi tape, each 60 cm long, and place them 10 cm apart on the game, as shown.

8. Now cut five 10-cm strips of tape and place them across the two longer pieces of tape. Create two more ladders in the same way and position them on the game, as shown on pages 204–205.

9. Using the green, yellow and red rolls of washi tape, copy the picture on the left to create three snakes. Position them on the game, as shown on pages 204–205.

## HOW TO PLAY
Roll the giant die from pages 208–209 to move around the game, and use plastic cups for counters. Don't forget to climb up the ladders and slide down the slippery snakes as you go!

## MATERIALS

black paper

cardboard

scissors    pencil    glue    all-purpose
                      stick    glue*      plastic cup

craft knife

cutting mat    metal ruler

## DIE TEMPLATE
(not to size)

5 cm

25 cm

25 cm

5 cm

5 cm

25 cm

25 cm    25 cm    25 cm

25 cm

* Ask an adult to help you use
  the all-purpose glue in step 4!

**1.**
Use a ruler and pencil to copy the
die template onto cardboard.

**2.**
Cut around the outer edge of the
template, using the craft knife and
ruler on a cutting mat. Now score
along the remaining pencil lines.*

* Ask an adult to help with this step.

**3.**
Fold along the scored lines and start
bending the cardboard into a cube.

**4.**
Add all-purpose glue to the tabs, then
stick them to the inside of the cube.
Hold each tab in place until set.

208

**5.**
Next, draw around the cup onto
black paper to create 21 circles.
Then cut them all out.

**6.**
Glue one circle to a side, then six
circles to the opposite side. Add two
circles to another side, then five circles
opposite. Add three circles to another
side, then four circles opposite.
Now you're ready to play!

IT'S DIE-NORMOUS!

# HULA
# HOOP
# RUG

**HULA YA CALLING RUGGED?**

Hula hoops are great for twirling around your body... and weaving! Use your favourite giant hoop as the frame loom for this chunky rug craft.

**MATERIALS**
hula hoop,
old cotton T-shirt,
wool,
rope (or twine),
pom-poms on thread,
scissors

**1.** Cut the T-shirt horizontally into long strips, stopping just beneath the sleeves (discard the bottom strip with the hem if it's not as stretchy as the rest). You will need at least eight strips.

**2.** Slide and stretch two of the strips across the hula hoop to form a cross, as shown.

**3.** Continue doing this until you have at least eight strips on the hoop. It should look a little bit like a bicycle wheel.

**4.** Now you're ready to start weaving the wool around the spokes. Tie a double knot in the wool at the centre of the rug, as shown.

**5.** Now weave the wool in and out of the spokes, pulling it tightly as you go.

**6.** Keep going around the spokes until you're ready to use another material (different-coloured wool, rope or pom-poms on thread).

**7.** When you're ready to switch material, tie one end of the new wool or material to the end of the wool already woven into the spokes.

**8.** Repeat steps 5 to 7, adding either the wool, rope or pom-poms, and continue to build up your rug.

**9.** Keep going until you're happy with the rug's size.

**10.** To remove the rug from the hoop, cut off the T-shirt spokes, as shown.

**11.** Continue until all the spokes are free and your rug is no longer attached to the hula hoop.

**12.** Now tuck the ends of a spoke over and through the last woven row of wool or material. Then pull it tight, as shown. This is called a lark's head knot.

**13.** Tie the ends together in a secure double knot. Repeat steps 12 to 13 on the other spokes.

**14.** Trim the spokes so they are all the same length. These are now the rug's tassels.

**15.** Add colour to the tassels by wrapping different-coloured wool around the top of each one.

**16.** Tie a double knot in the wool (around the back). Then your rug is ready to use!

# MATERIALS

sewing machine (optional),
pencil,
needle,
thread,
glue stick,
coloured card x 16
(10 cm x 10 cm),
buttons x 16,
scissors,
eraser,
white card (45 cm x 45 cm)

**1.** Draw a stick person in the middle of a piece of coloured card, leaving the head area blank, as shown.

**2.** Starting at the stick person's neck, sew straight lines along the pencil marks using the sewing machine. Keep the needle in the down position and lift the presser foot to change direction as you go. Continue stitching around the stick person until you return to the start, then trim the thread ends.

**3.** Sew a button to the top of the stick person's neck (for the head). Tie a double knot at the back of the card to secure the button head in place.

**4.** Use the eraser to remove any pencil lines. Repeat steps 1 to 3 until you have 16 cards of stick people in different kinds of action poses. Now glue the cards onto the white card and frame your stick-tastic creations!

READY, SET...
**SEW!**

# ON-A-ROLL ADVENT CALENDAR

COUNTDOWN TO CHRISTMAS!

## MATERIALS

scissors

stamp pad

wrapped sweets x 25

white glue

toilet rolls x 25*

white card

glue stick

number stamps

1 2 3
4 5 6
7 8 9
0

pencil

ribbon

light green and red tissue paper

* Ask an adult to microwave the toilet rolls for 30 seconds to get rid of any germs before use!

1 cm

**1.** Draw around the bottom of a toilet roll onto white card. Sketch a circle that is 1 cm bigger around the one you've just drawn, then cut it out. This is your template.

**2.** Use the template to draw 32 circles onto the green tissue paper (half of these will cover the top of the toilet roll, and the other half will cover the bottom).

2

1

**3.** Now draw 18 circles onto the red tissue paper (again, half will cover the top, while the rest will cover the bottom). Then cut out the green and red circles.

**4.** Take 9 red circles and 16 green circles, then stamp a number from 1 to 25 on each one (printing each number only once).

217

**5.** Take a plain (unnumbered) red circle, and run the glue stick around the edges.

**6.** Place a toilet roll in the middle of the circle.

**7.** Stick down the edges, as shown, then repeat steps 5 to 7 on more toilet rolls to create 16 plain red-ended rolls and 9 plain green-ended rolls.

**8.** Put a wrapped sweet in each roll. Cover the front with a numbered circle, matching the colour to the plain one on the other end.

**9.** When all the rolls have been covered, get ready to glue them together in rows of five.

**10.** First, add white glue to one side of a red-ended roll.

**11.** Gently push the glued edge against another red-ended roll. Then hold in place for a few minutes to help the glue to stick.

**12.** Repeat until five red rolls are joined together.

**13.** Glue one red-ended and four green-ended rolls together, as shown. Add glue on the top of each roll. Repeat for the remaining rolls, but leave the last row unglued along the top.

**14.** Now glue all the rows on top of each other, with the red rolls forming a cross in the middle, as shown.

**15.** Once dry, wrap some ribbon around the outside of the rolls and tie a double knot on top.

**16.** Make a bow, then tie the two loose ends together tightly so that the calendar can be hung up. Roll on Christmas!

# NEON NOTE
# MONSTERS

## MATERIALS
square neon sticky notes in 4 colours
black marker pen

LET'S STICK
TOGETHER!

1. Clean a large wall space, ready for your work of art.*

2. Hold a note with the sticky edge at the top. Now place it on the wall, starting at the top left. Do the same with the other notes, going from left to right, working your way down to the floor.

3. Keep looking at the picture on the right while you add each note.

4. When you have completed your pop art monster mural, draw on some black dots for the monsters' eyes, to finish.

\* The sticky notes are easy to remove and unlikely to damage paint or papered surfaces. However, we recommend you ask an adult's permission first and test a small area before you start.

# INDEX